12

مهه

996

BETWEEN
REALISM and
REALITY

The Reagan Administration and International Debt

James W. Joseph
University of Texas, Tyler

UNIVERSITY
PRESS OF
AMERICA

Lanham • New York • London

University Press of America®, Inc.
4720 Boston Way
Lanham, Maryland 20706

3 Henrietta Street
London WC2E 8LU England

All rights reserved
Printed in the United States of America
British Cataloging in Publication Information Available

Library of Congress Cataloging-in-Publication Data

Joseph, James W.
Between realism and reality : the Reagan administration
and international debt / James W. Joseph.
    p.   cm.
Includes bibliographical references and index.
1. Debts, External.   2. United States—Foreign economic
relations.   3. International finance.   I. Title.
HJ8015.J67   1993   336.3'435—dc20   93–28911 CIP

ISBN 0–8191–9274–0 (cloth : alk. paper)
ISBN 0–8191–9275–9 (pbk. : alk. paper)

 The paper used in this publication meets the minimum requirements of American National Standard for Information Sciences—Permanence of Paper for Printed Library Materials, ANSI Z39.48–1984.

TABLE OF CONTENTS

iv

LIST OF TABLES

vi

LIST OF FIGURES

Permission to reprint from Pedro-Pablo Kuczynski, Latin American Debt (Baltimore: Johns Hopkins University Press, 1988) is acknowledged.

Permission to reprint from Robert O. Keohane and Joseph S. Nye, Power and Interdependence: World Politics in Transition (Boston: Little, Brown, 1977; Glenview [IL]: Scott, Foresman, 1989 [second edition]) is acknowledged from Harper Collins Publishers.

CHAPTER ONE

INTRODUCTION: PUZZLES AND POLICIES

In early 1987 it was estimated that Third World states collectively owed over one trillion dollars to foreign creditors. This external debt translated into approximately $250 per person owed either to foreign governments, the International Monetary Fund (IMF), multilateral development banks (MDBs) such as the World Bank and its affiliated agencies, and private commercial banks (Bouchet, 1987:xv,3). This situation is the legacy of the international debt explosion which started with the petrodollar recycling following the 1973-74 oil price shocks.

Figure One and Table One indicate the magnitude of the increase in external debt held by less developed countries (LDCs). It is quickly apparent that the debt "overhang" for the Third World is large, and burgeoning, in aggregate terms. These funds are owed by a large number of countries, with varied political and economic characteristics; most of them have experienced tremendous growth in their external debt within the last decade.

It has also been obvious to developing states, and to some external creditors, that real problems have resulted from the need to finance debt payments. As the necessary funds must be found somewhere, fiscally strapped governments have cut back or cancelled varieties of projects. Industrialization programs are often slowed or halted, and social services are reduced. In the end, it is quite possible a connection exists between the economic situation in LDCs and the type and effectiveness of their governments. For example, in Latin America some observers worry about the viability of fledgling democracies if the need to make debt payments squeezes public expenditures.[1] There is concern that even states with long records of peaceful democracy may be threatened; among Latin American countries, for example, Costa Rica has the highest per capita external debt (Wiarda, 1988:120).

Concerns about external debts and the prospects of sovereign debtor default are not new in international finance. But the size and severity of the present burden are unsurpassed:

The feeling of déjá vu, however, is lessened today by the global dimension and the far-reaching implications of the less developed countries' external financial problems. The debt crisis represents the end of the prolonged and widespread growth cycle of the postwar period. The magnitude of the crisis; the interactions between financial, economic, and sociopolitical factors; and the interdependence between participants suggest altogether that the situation is not merely a cyclical and temporary downturn in liquidity, trade, and growth. Rather, the debt problem is leading to a structural change in the world economy with long-run implications for the interactions between poles of growth, for economic and political leadership, and for role distribution on the international scene (Bouchet, 1987:xvii).

FIGURE 1

**Total Developing Country Debt and Proportion of
Bank Involvement, 1979-1987**

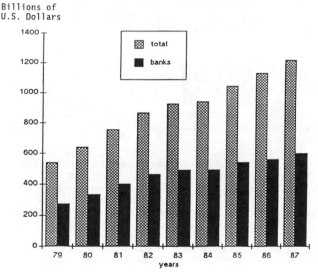

Source: BIS; IMF; World Bank. Cited in Bouchet, 1987:3.

These problems may call into question a wide array of assumptions about global economics, including those of established Keynesian macroeconomic wisdom. This change, as yet incomplete, could be as dramatic as the further decline of the "gold standard, the balance-of-power system, and the self-regulating market" which Polanyi (1957) saw as existing only until the late nineteenth or early twentieth centuries (Bouchet, 1987:xvii).

Clearly, then, the way in which international debt is arranged and amortized has much to do with the shape of the international economic system. But it is also relevant to the structure and processes of the international political system. International relations theorists writing in various "traditions" assume different features of the international system, and of the actors within it. According to Holsti (1985:15-81), there are three broad theoretical trends in international relations: realism, dependency, and global society approaches. "Realists" assume an anarchic international system, in which conflict is a continual possibility, and in which nation-states inevitably act to guard their political and economic power. Dependency theorists, who borrow substantially from Marxist writings, see the international system as dominated mainly by capitalist economic forces. For them, nation-states are divided primarily into the "have" states of the industrial, bourgeois "center" to which economic wealth and power flow; and the "have-not" countries of the underdeveloped "periphery", from which

TABLE 1

Total Long-Term Public and Private External Debt as Percentage of GNP--Top Twenty Debtor Countries

Country	1970	1984
Mauritania	13.9%	171.2%
Nicaragua	14.8	141.8
Zambia	37.5	115.4
Costa Rica	25.3	114.0
Jamaica	92.8	108.8
Bolivia	36.1	108.7
Ivory Coast	19.1	107.5
Yemen PDR	--	106.9
Chile	32.1	100.2
Togo	16.0	100.1
Israel	47.9	99.5
Mali	88.1	95.9
Papua New Guinea	33.4	78.1
Liberia	49.9	77.4
Sudan	15.2	77.2
Nigeria	--	76.7
Congo, People's Rep.	53.9	76.2
Ecuador	14.7	75.1
Panama	19.5	73.3
Tanzania	20.7	69.6

Source: World Bank Development Report 1986, Table 17. Cited in Darity and Horn, 1988:182.

money, resources, and human capital are siphoned. This is generally a parasitic relationship. Global society writers view the international system as one increasingly dominated by pressing environmental, social, and economic issues which are not amenable to solution by individual nation-states. This implies the need to create supranational organizations which can effectively deal with problems either ignored by the international state system, or dealt with ineffectively.

The history of international debt in the last decade, however, cannot be adequately conceptualized under any one of these analytic frameworks. Realist literature is state-centric, assuming nation-states as the main actors in international affairs. But the variety of salient actors in the international debt issue area includes states, multilateral organizations, private banks, and powerful individuals. Neither would realism anticipate the marked degree of cooperation among the myriad actors since the debt "crisis"[2] started in the early 1980s. While dependency writers see LDCs as largely lacking in political and economic power, debtor states have demonstrated both an understanding of the international economic forces that have brought them to their present situation, and the capacity for organizing themselves to seek a greater voice in debt negotiations. Few observers would completely rule out the possibility of debtor nations declaring a moratorium on payments. Scholars in the global society school would expect states to recognize the need for international organizations to address problems of mounting debt and repayment difficulties, but the multilateral bodies active in debt have been given comparatively little power by their state members. In addition, these states have shown few signs of recognizing a changing global agenda of issues and concerns.

In short, international debt as a political, economic, and social issue reflects substantial changes in the structure of and processes within the international system, and more specifically within the international political economy. It therefore requires innovation in how scholars study this subject.

As the following chapters will illustrate, the United States has been active in the international debt issue area in the last decade. As such, debt is a vital topic of study because it provides a perspective on U.S. foreign policy. At issue are such matters as the U.S.'s role as a global systemic leader, and how foreign policy decision making is conducted in the U.S. As to the first topic, much debate has taken place in international relations theory of late about the U.S.'s role as the military and economic hegemon of the "First World" capitalist, industrial countries. Discussion has centered on whether the U.S. is declining or holding steady as a hegemon, and what the implications are of either. As it relates to the present topic, such thinkers have an interest in knowing whether the U.S. has been a leader or a follower on management of the debt situation, and should be expected to ask how this relates to the theory of hegemonic stability (see Gilpin, 1981) in general, and its validity within distinct issue areas.

On the second topic, the international debt dilemma reveals patterns of decision making within the U.S. government (recognizing that these patterns are at least partly the result of idiosyncratic factors within particular presidential administrations). A careful investigation of policy making can show which officials were involved, when they took an active role, and on which issues they participated. Such research also can illustrate the type of topics that get on the policy agenda, when and why they do so, and how issues rank in importance.

International debt, then, is at the junction of three broad, vital areas of study: 1) LDC development, 2) international political economy, and 3) foreign policy (especially American policy). External debt could be profitably studied from the standpoint of any of these three subjects; the most accurate picture, however, would probably be gained from the study of all three.

Reagan and Debt Policy

There are theoretical and policy-oriented reasons to study international debt from these three perspectives. However, without intending to ignore what may be the most important facet of the external debt situation--the human and social costs for LDCs--the following chapters focus on a "puzzle" found in the last category. Specifically, an attempt will be made to explain Reagan Administration debt policy from 1981 to 1985.

In four cases, the Administration did not act as it would have been expected, given the rhetoric used in the 1980 presidential campaign, and the public statements of Administration officials once in power. It also did not act in accordance with its stated policies regarding debtor countries, MDBs, private commercial banks, and other creditor governments. Lastly, it violated its own assumptions about the international political economy, and what was required of the U.S. as a political and economic superpower.

The four cases were:

Poland. Throughout its first year in office, the Reagan Administration watched closely the developing labor strife in Poland, as the Solidarity labor union continued to grow in power. The U.S. often signalled the Soviet Union that any intervention in Poland would further chill U.S.-Soviet ties, which had already deteriorated since before Reagan took office. In December 1981 the Polish government declared martial law, causing the Administration to impose economic sanctions on Poland. Many observers claimed these measures were of little impact. Some in the Administration believed the U.S. had found a better way to punish Poland when in early 1982 the Polish government was unable to make interest payments on millions of dollars of Agriculture Department credits. Discussion in the Administration revolved around two options: 1) to declare Poland in default on its obligations, which would hopefully force the Soviet Union to come to its aid and indirectly sanction the Soviets for the crackdown, or 2) to heed the calls from the U.S.'s European allies to renegotiate or reschedule Poland's payments. The Administration finally decided on the second course, and quietly paid some of the debts itself, to avoid further discord between the U.S. and its allies.

Mexico. In August 1982, Mexico declared itself unable to make further payments on its mounting external debt, and asked the U.S. and the IMF for assistance in rescheduling its payments. The Reagan Administration, which had spent much of the previous year and a half touting the virtues of the global free market and the need for LDCs to stand on their own in devising development plans, uncharacteristically took the lead in preventing international economic "meltdown". The U.S. quickly arranged to loan $2 billion to Mexico, and became a vital actor in the IMF's bailout plan; the Administration also took its most active position to that point in the Bank for International Settlements' (BIS) discussions on the "crisis".

The IMF Quota Increase. In late 1982 the Reagan Administration, along with the governments of other nations, agreed to a substantial increase in the size of members' quotas for the IMF. The Administration had previously expressed great skepticism about the value of international organizations as a tool for developing Third World states. Yet after the IMF had taken a major role in preventing the Mexican default, and had done the same with Brazil just a few months later, the Administration accepted a plan to increase by nearly 50% American deposits with the organization. Throughout most of 1983 the Administration pushed its funding request through Congress, against solid opposition from both liberals and conservatives. Only by making major concessions to opponents was the Administration able to prevail.

The Baker Plan. In late 1985, in response to further deterioration in the economic position of major debtor states, Treasury Secretary James Baker announced a three-part plan for defusing the international debt "bomb". The U.S., he proposed, would dramatically increase its lending to developing countries, if private commercial banks would do the same, and if LDCs would adopt more free market means of conducting business and trade. Baker's program focused on fifteen of the most heavily indebted countries. This serves as the final case in this study, because it most clearly represents the official recognition by the Administration that its previous debt policy had not been successful in reducing the risk of major defaults.

In January 1981, the Reagan Administration entered office with Reagan and his advisors saying that the U.S. would act "realistically", both in politics and economics. In economics, for example, Reagan talked of the "magic of the marketplace", in which all states and individuals can and should be allowed to compete freely for advantages. The Administration consistently argued for little or no government intervention in international (and domestic) economics, on the belief that "international policy coordination" (Keohane and Nye, 1985:149) would not foster efficiency and growth. International organizations, the Reagan approach maintained, were largely inimical to capitalism; their political bent was too socialist and they too freely and unwisely mixed the political and social agendas of LDCs with Keynesian economic theory.

By late 1982, however, the Administration had allowed political considerations to take precedence over economic ones in the cases of Poland and Mexico. The Administration had taken a more active role in managing the international debt situation than would have been expected, dramatically increasing its participation in the BIS and the Paris Club[3]. It embraced--albeit grudgingly--the IMF as an important actor in debt management after the Mexican bailout, and fought hard throughout 1983 to get the U.S.'s IMF quota raised. Just two years later in the Baker Plan it made plain its conviction that international debt difficulties would not disappear on their own.

The four cases on which this study focuses are benchmarks. That is, they were the most obvious Administration action taken at particular times. What follows is not meant as a report on the day-to-day activities of the Administration, but instead a look at its policies in certain periods. The time frame of this project therefore covers early Administration policy, when international debt was not seen as crucial, to the advent of the Baker Plan, when the U.S. conceded that laissez-faire approaches to debt had not only not solved the debt problem, but may in fact have worsened it.

Assuming that puzzles exist--that committed policy makers did not act as they desired, or as they were expected, in an issue area where they anticipated much freedom for the U.S. to maneuver--how can these mysteries be explained? Assuming that the Administration's goals were consistent with a "realist's" conception of the subject area--which I will deal with in Chapter Two--one is left to ask how this divergence between proposed and actual policies can be understood.

Taking a "level of analysis" approach developed by Waltz (1959) and advanced to "pre-theory" status for comparative foreign policy purposes by Rosenau (1966), it is possible to assess how different factors could be used to explain Reagan policies. Kegley and Wittkopf (1987) use the five following levels to explain U.S. foreign policies; here they are applied to international debt.

As for the individual and role levels, it is impossible to conclusively rule out a massive change in the way in which Reagan Administration officials perceived either the subject, or their jobs within the government, between the time they took office and the time difficult decisions had to be made about debt. Another difficulty is that many techniques for studying decision making by policy makers are inadequate without access to corroborating documentary evidence. Nonetheless, certain facts are clear. It will be shown that Administration policy grew progressively less "hard-line" about debt. Officials usually found themselves reacting to situations; they were unable to get ahead of problems. Of the policy shifts which occurred, many of them took place early in the Administration's tenure, among the original hard-line individuals; it is plain that the changes in the way the Administration acted were not due solely to shifts in personnel. As to the impact of roles, there is little to indicate any pronounced shift in the goals Reagan officials set for themselves, their agencies, and the U.S, especially within the first two to three years.

Attempts to explain the shift in Administration debt policy at the governmental and societal levels also prove inadequate. Most of the action on debt policy took place within the executive branch, without a great deal of input from other branches of the government, the public, or the media. Only on the IMF quota increase is this not completely true, and even here the congressional and public outcry against additional funds for the IMF was muted and did not result in the Administration losing its fight for an increased U.S. quota.

The shift in Administration policy is best explained at the systemic level. It is manifest that the U.S. did not find the international distribution of power, at least in the international debt area, as it expected or hoped. Realist assumptions within international relations theory would assume a certain "fungibility" to power, so that U.S. strength in other policy areas would be translated into capabilities in debt policy. Such were the assumptions held by Reagan officials. The reality, however, was that the U.S. could not dictate other actors' courses of action regarding external debt, and had difficulty at times even leading such policies. Consequently, the international debt management scheme which began to emerge after Mexico's near default in 1982 only partially resembled the one the Reagan Administration would have created. What is needed, then, to explain U.S. policy is a system-level approach that accurately captures the systemic distribution of capabilities in international debt during the period in question.

Complex Interdependence

In 1977 Robert O. Keohane and Joseph S. Nye published Power and Interdependence: World Politics In Transition. Within a short period of time this book was widely read and discussed both in and out of the field of international relations, because of the attention it gave to shifting patterns of world politics and economics, and the suggestions it made for the theoretical analysis of these trends. The impact of Power and Interdependence was so great within the field that Keohane and

Nye's text became the "exemplar" of one of two intellectual "variants" within behavioral international relations theory at the time (Alker and Biersteker, 1984:123-127). Their framework helps explain Reagan Administration debt policies.

Keohane and Nye portray the international system as increasingly characterized by "complex interdependence", in which assumptions of realist literature about 1) what actors have impact in global affairs, 2) which issues are dominant, and 3) what constitutes power, are no longer inevitably valid. In fact, there are three qualities of the structure of power in international relations that reflect the existence of complex interdependence. First, there are multiple channels of contact; by this Keohane and Nye indicate an increasing variety of actors have influence in world politics. These actors are both governmental and nongovernmental, and differ by issue area, making for still more actors which must be recognized by state officials. Second, there is an absence of hierarchy among issues. Unlike the situation assumed in most realist writing, in which the concern over national security is paramount for decision-makers, in complex interdependence a variety of issues may take precedence on the policy agenda. States may become interdependent in a number of ways, making national security less central in their calculations. Third, there is a minor role for military force. Ties of interdependence among states--both allies and competitors--make the use of violence less of an option than in previous times. Not only would military power in pursuit of objectives do damage usually out of proportion to the goals sought, but such measures would inevitably harm relations across the spectrum of issue areas on which nation-states have ties. As a result, power no longer exists strictly in military terms; it is more contingent on the situation and issue area at hand.

Not only does the structure and distribution of power in the international system in conditions of complex interdependence differ from those found in realist conditions, but the processes of political interaction have changed as well. For example, because power is situational, states are not able to link issues as readily as in times past; success in one issue area does not imply success in another. Because of the absence of a set hierarchy of issues, "agenda formation and control will become more important" (Keohane and Nye, 1977:32), and the policy agenda within states will not always be determined by the international distribution of power, and shifts in that balance. Keohane and Nye also find that there has been and will continue to be an increase in the role and salience of transnational and transgovernmental actors; this is accompanied by a reduction in the differences between external and domestic politics, since many of these actors operate on both levels. Finally, as a result of the increase in channels of contact among actors, international organizations have gained in significance; the ease of LDCs in getting roles in such organizations has and will cause substantial changes in the foci of these bodies, and the way they conduct business.

Keohane and Nye apply their framework to the political processes found in the issue areas of monetary affairs and oceans space and resources, because the "continued importance" of these subjects "from the nineteenth century to the present allows [them] to test the applicability" of complex interdependence "under changing political and economic conditions" (1977:63). They also assess the bilateral relationships between the U.S. and Canada and between the U.S. and Australia in the five decades after 1920. They choose the U.S.-Canada dyad as an ideal case in which to find complex interdependence, because of the close, mutually dependent relationships between the two countries. The U.S.-Australia dyad is selected because Australia allows for holding "constant the effects of size, general economic characteristics, and domestic political systems", while the authors "look at the effects of differences in the two countries' military security and at the costly effects of geographical distance" (1977:166). Keohane and Nye find that realist assumptions explain the conditions in the oceans and monetary affairs regimes reasonably well in the first four decades under study; after that the complex interdependence explanation is more appropriate. They also find both pre-World War II dyadic relationships, and the postwar U.S.-Australia relationship, as better understood by realism, but the postwar U.S.-Canada one as more appropriately understood as one of complex interdependence. As a result of their case studies, Keohane and Nye are able to draw conclusions about when realist and complex interdependence approaches are more likely to apply in specific issue areas, and in international politics generally.

The goals of <u>Power and Interdependence</u> are limited. Keohane and Nye do not seek (as some writers have) to deny completely the validity of realism as a set of assumptions about the structure and processes of international politics. Realism accurately conceptualizes events in some situations and at certain times, they admit; the authors do however seek to note under which conditions realist approaches are inaccurate. To achieve their objectives, they develop both realism and complex interdependence as "ideal types", and acknowledge that "most situations will fall somewhere between the two extremes" (1977:24), hence often neither by itself is a fully satisfactory approach. In addition, despite the dyadic studies, the book is aimed at the systemic level, with little attention paid to other levels of analysis, or to the matter of how the international system reached its present situation.

Despite its shortcomings, complex interdependence as an analytic framework can be applied to the structure of power in the international debt management regime[4] within the last decade. A number of features of the politics of that regime appear relevant.

For example, the assortment of actors, and the way they interact regarding debt, reflect multiple channels of contact. There is perhaps a wider array of participants in debt discussions than on any other issue of global economic importance. The list includes creditor governments, debtor governments, MDBs, other international organizations, private commercial banks, and a multitude of subnational state agencies. Most of these actors have particular objectives which they pursue in international debt, and there is no guarantee that their goals are in line with those of any other actor. Particular governmental departments are known to address their own concerns even if those goals conflict with the desires of other state agencies. This fact is even more pronounced between entirely different actors, or classes of actors; banks, for example, have become "full participants in the realm of foreign policy", as largely independent actors whose interests may not correspond to those of their home governments and publics (Cohen, 1985:128).

The lack of an obvious hierarchy of issues has also appeared in international debt. Evidence indicates that the external debt situation has been a major concern for a large number of both LDCs and developed states; at the same time territorial security has not been an issue. A close inspection of the literature on external debt shows that many actors, both in times of "crisis" such as the Mexican near default, and in less worrisome times, saw debt as the crucial issue facing the international economy. All other matters were secondary in consequence. Within debt policies themselves, moreover, military and territorial security considerations not only did not get to compete with other concerns, they were never even considered.

Finally, it is clear that the role for military force has been quite limited in international debt negotiations. Creditor states and banks seem to have assumed that military activity would be of little use in attempting to compel payments from debtors, and the use of such measures would be inordinately expensive financially and politically, in both the short and long terms.

Not only does the structure of capabilities within international debt reflect conditions of complex interdependence, but so do the processes of interaction. Because power within discussions regarding external debt has proven to be contingent upon the particular conditions which apply at the time, actors have found it difficult to link arrangements in debt to agreements in other areas; it is even sometimes a formidable task to trade political favors within debt negotiations. As the conditions of complex interdependence would expect, national policy agendas have become more influenced by myriad nongovernmental actors, whose successes have had little to do with their "power" as it has been traditionally understood. Also as might be expected, international organizations have gained in importance in global affairs, because LDCs have used these bodies as forums to discuss the debt situation, and to debate debtor options.

Keohane and Nye develop complex interdependence as a condition of the international system, at least in specific instances. How can this approach be applied to the foreign policy of a particular country? More to the point, how can the Reagan Administration's actions on international debt be explained from a complex interdependence interpretation? To do so, it is necessary to develop a framework of foreign policy in issue areas where complex interdependence is found. That is, it is essential to show that conditions in international debt were such that the Reagan Administration did not have many options in dealing with the debt "crisis".

Chapters Four and Five are devoted to this purpose. Chapter Four illustrates the structure of political power, and the processes of interaction, within the oceans and monetary affairs issue areas. Chapter Five then compares these with external debt as an issue area, and establishes that international debt resembles the complex interdependence found in the recent oceans and money regimes. I then seek to devise from the structural characteristics and the political processes of complex interdependence a set of expectations for foreign policy in such a situation. These expectations will then be used to explain Reagan debt policy in the four cases outlined earlier.

Goals

International debt is itself a broad and deep topic, with a number of different subcategories. As I indicated earlier, it is also at the junction of important, wider areas of study. Nevertheless, the goals involved in what follows actually are rather narrow and pertain to a discrete subject matter; if any conclusions can be drawn about material or issues outside the main focus of this work, they are unintended.

The main purpose here is to explain Reagan Administration policies on international debt, by way of concentrating on the four particular cases mentioned above. This focus involves a recognizable policy area as yet largely untouched in the literature. Also relatively ignored has been the question of to what extent the Reagan understanding of the international system was "realist", and whether an alternative set of assumptions about this environment were more accurate. The following chapters deal with these questions.

A number of secondary goals exist as well. On the subject of U.S. foreign policy, this project provides an opportunity to ask in what other issue areas besides international debt complex interdependence could be found. From this, some thought will be given to the likely future of U.S. foreign policy, if topics similar to international debt can be located. As for international relations theory, the following chapters may stimulate discussion about the general validity of Keohane and Nye's framework, and hopefully go some distance toward developing a conceptual (but not yet explanatory) model of foreign policy in conditions of complex interdependence (or simply "interdependence").

There are limits to what this study is intended to accomplish. For example, it is not designed as a "kiss-and-tell" exposition about the decision-makers in the Administration. Such books are usually devoid of any useful theoretical conclusions, and do not lend themselves to corroborative replication. Nor does this text attempt to create a psychological profile of Administration decision makers in hopes of explaining policy choices. As was stated earlier, such an attempt would require a great deal more detailed information about internal Administration dealings, in a variety of policy areas, than has been available until just recently.

Some other restrictions about the purposes of this study are worth noting. This project is not an attempt to elevate complex interdependence to the status of an international relations paradigm. One reason is that Keohane and Nye themselves do not consider such an attempt wise or necessary; another is that the fundamental features of complex interdependence are not sufficiently distinctive to warrant such an attempt. (See Chapter Ten for further discussion.) This study also does not undertake to draw conclusions about other Reagan foreign policies; it overtly adopts the assumption made by Keohane and Nye that some issues are most effectively evaluated with regard to the distribution of capabilities existing within those issue areas. Finally, this is not an attempt to discuss the history of the debt "crisis"; there are numerous very good texts on the subject already.[5]

For all that the following chapters do not attempt, the entire text does deal with three topics that individually and collectively make the focus herein valuable. First, it deals with the structure and governing rules of the international system, and the international political economy; also at issue is the way in which scholars understand these subjects. Second, it investigates issues involved in U.S. foreign policy making, and the position of the U.S. as a political and economic power. Third, and at least in some limited sense, it is concerned with the status of the economies in LDCs, and their development plans. The first topic may be of interest primarily to academics, and the second will be of concern mainly to scholars and the politically curious. But the final focus may be of consequence to a very diverse, broad group-- those with an interest in a basic issue involving a considerable portion of humanity.

Chapter Outline

The remaining chapters are structured in the following fashion. Chapters Two through Five deal primarily with theoretical matters. Chapter Two begins by relating the dominance of realism within international relations study, and evaluates Reagan Administration claims to be acting realistically. Chapter Three then looks at <u>Power and Interdependence</u>, and the concept of complex interdependence, as an attempt to challenge part of realism's dominance within international relations. Chapter Four summarizes Keohane and Nye's history of the oceans and monetary affairs regimes. Chapter Five explains how the power structure and political processes found in international debt closely resemble those found in the most recent oceans and money regimes, where conditions of complex interdependence are most obvious. It then moves on to the development of a set of characteristics expected in the foreign policy of states finding themselves having to act in issue areas characterized by complex interdependence.

Chapters Six through Nine concentrate on the cases under review. Chapter Six centers on U.S. policy on Poland in 1981 and 1982, when the Reagan Administration found itself caught between its political desires and economic constraints. Chapter Seven reviews the Mexican bailout in late 1982, and the effect of the barely-avoided disaster on Administration thinking about international economics. Chapter Eight follows the Administration's decision to support a general capital increase for the IMF, and its campaign to get Congress to appropriate funds for the U.S. share. Chapter Nine examines the genesis of the Baker Plan, and its presentation to the major actors in the debt management regime.

Chapter Ten offers a summary of findings and some conclusions. It evaluates the success of the analytic framework designed in Chapter Five, advances a research agenda on additional tests for this approach, and closes with some comments on the status of the international debt situation now.

Endnotes

[1]See for example Barbara Stallings and Robert Kaufman, eds., Debt and Democracy in Latin America, Boulder: Westview Press, 1989.

[2]Throughout the remainder of this study I will refrain from discussing the international debt situation as a "crisis". Perhaps the only time when the use of such a term was appropriate was in late 1982, when a distinct possibility existed of LDCs declaring a payments moratorium. This term has been overused, especially in the popular press; it implies some juncture at which the international debt problem must be resolved in one fashion or another. Obviously, a condition which has persisted this long does not really qualify as a "crisis", despite its seriousness.

[3]The Paris Club is the ad hoc forum in which major creditor states work with LDCs to reschedule the latter's external debt. The London Club is a companion forum for the rescheduling of LDC debt owed to commercial banks.

[4]Benjamin J. Cohen provides an early suggestion that the international debt situation, especially in regards the rise of new actors, may correspond to a complex interdependence framework. See "International Debt and Linkage Strategies: Some Foreign Policy Implications for the United States", in Miles Kahler, ed. The Politics of International Debt, Ithaca: Cornell University Press, 1986.

[5]A comprehensive list of books on the debt "crisis" would of course be lengthy, but there are some especially insightful ones. Included are Michel Henri Bouchet, The Political Economy of International Debt: What, Who, How Much, and Why? New York: Quorum Books, 1987; Miles Kahler, ed. The Politics of International Debt, Ithaca: Cornell University Press, 1986; Brian Kettell and George Magnus, The International Debt Game, London: Graham and Trotman Limited, 1986; John H. Makin, The Global Debt Crisis: America's Growing Involvement, New York: Basic Books, 1984; Jeffrey D. Sachs, ed. Developing Country Debt and the World Economy, Chicago: University of Chicago Press, 1989; Barbara Stallings, Banker to the Third World: U.S. Portfolio Investment in Latin America, 1900-1986, Berkeley: University of California Press, 1987; Robert Wesson, ed. Coping With the Latin American Debt, New York: Praeger, 1988.

CHAPTER TWO

REALISM AND THE REAGAN ADMINISTRATION

It is fair to associate Ronald Reagan with "realism" in foreign policy. He campaigned for the presidency in 1980 on the virtues of this outlook in foreign affairs, and promised his presidential policies would reflect this approach. Other officials in his administration reiterated this desire; in fact, their knowledge of what realism would entail in specific policy areas may have made them more effective advocates than the President.

One of its goals, the Reagan team said, was not to repeat the actions of the Carter Administration. Reagan officials believed Jimmy Carter had needlessly presided over Soviet-sponsored insurgencies in Africa, had done little to answer the Soviet invasion of Afghanistan, and had refused to respond to increasing repression in Poland. Carter was also seen as too dependent on socialist-leaning international organizations like the IMF and World Bank to pursue goals the U.S could achieve unilaterally, or in close contact with its western allies. In short, Jimmy Carter had needlessly weakened the U.S., both politically and economically.

Notwithstanding its rhetoric, Reagan Administration policy on international debt does not fit well within the realist framework its officials espoused. The explanation advanced here is that the Administration found a substantially different international system than it had expected, at least--perhaps especially--in the external debt structure.

To test these assertions, and to develop an alternative explanation, four things must be done. First, it must be clearly stated what is meant by "realism". Second, it is necessary to show that the original Reagan goals fell comfortably within this oategory. Third, it is necessary to explain Keohane and Nye's substitute approach to systemic politics. Finally, to test the claims of this book it is necessary to devise a model of foreign policy from Keohane and Nye's characteristics of complex interdependence.

This chapter is devoted to the first and second of these tasks. It profiles realism as a body of literature in international relations, and as a framework for understanding foreign policy. It then compares the assumptions behind Reagan policies with those expected from an ideal type of realist policy maker; this helps to locate Administration objectives in the realist mode. Chapter Three discusses Keohane and Nye's Power and Interdependence and their concepts of complex interdependence as features of the international system. Chapters Four and Five concentrate on complex interdependence and its affect on foreign policies in the oceans and money issue areas, and then elaborate on a conceptual model of these policies against which Reagan debt policy can be measured.

Realism in Theory and Practice

It would be difficult to deny that realism--whether called "realism", "the classical tradition" (Holsti, 1985), "traditionalism" (Maghroori and Ramberg, 1982), or something else--is the most dominant approach to global politics in the field of international relations. It almost certainly is the intellectual home for the largest number of theorists of world affairs, and contains the greatest variety of theoretical offshoots of any school of thought in the field. It also has the longest history of generally recognized "paradigms" in the discipline, and is the usual training ground for a majority of foreign policy makers, at least in the U.S. It is not surprising, then, that many politicians, including Reagan officials, would look within this framework for ways to conceptualize global affairs, and for suggested policies.

It would be superfluous to belabor what is a well-known approach for most scholars in international relations. Therefore, what follows is not intended as anything more elaborate than a brief sketch of realism's fundamental features. The purpose here is to point out 1) the reasons for occasional attempts by realism's critics to challenge its validity, and to replace it, and 2) the roots of Administration goals.

Realism in Theory

Briefly defined, realism can be understood as an interpretation of world politics in which conflict among sovereign states is always a source of concern, "power" is primarily (but not exclusively) military in nature, and the international system is unregulated by any ordering body. In realist discourse, the international system is often termed one of "self-help" (Waltz, 1979); states can look to no one but themselves as guarantors of peace and security. Dougherty and Pfaltzgraff (1981:2-10) have focused on the growth of international relations and realism; the succeeding passages borrow substantially from their synopsis of realism's growth.

The study of international politics is quite old; instances of such endeavors can even be found prior to the establishment of the present state system. Among the earliest recorded studies is Thucydides' account of the conflict between Athens and Sparta in History of the Peloponnesian War. Other writers on conflict and statecraft in pre-modern times were found in India (Modelski, 1964) and China. Realism's dominance as a framework for analysis and as a prescription for action is not too surprising, in that much of realist thought in the twentieth century has appeared before in various guises. Thucydides, for example, dealt with the uses of power and military force as means of policy. In The Prince, Machiavelli discussed his techniques of statecraft and advocated a dispassionate analysis of the developing state system; he analyzed the use of power to solve state problems and gain personal stature for its leaders. In more recent times, philosophers such as Rousseau, Bentham, Kant, and Grotius all experienced difficulties in attempting to design organizations to enforce international order. In the nineteenth century especially, the Napoleonic Wars seemed to lend credence to a pessimistic view of the likelihood of conflict among states.[1] Napoleon's attempt to remake the state system by military means gave support to those who argued that force needed to be met with force, and that it was unwise to trust in the goodwill of others. The apparent (if overstated) success of the "Concert" system in the years after France's defeat seemed to back up this interpretation. The success of balance of power politics[2] as a method for governing the system and insuring peace (or at least managing change) seemed to provide confirmation that the international state system was inherently competitive, with conflict always a risk, and that the best way to avoid another major threat to the system was for decision makers to have a healthy suspicion of other actors, and to maintain sufficient strength to prevent conflict. Such was the dominant interpretation of global politics among policy makers in 1914, at the start of the world war: force was usable, at relatively low or at least reasonable costs; leaders could speak for and control their states' foreign policies, and hence the shape of the world. War, in short, was merely a policy option.

But the experience of the First World War stimulated questioning of the generally accepted wisdom about world politics. Soon after the war ended, "realists" found themselves engaged in a debate with "idealists", a group of often brilliant, committed thinkers who opposed what they saw as the mind set that had launched the world's most costly armed struggle. These idealists (or "utopians" as some labeled them) claimed that a careful look at history showed that violent conflict was not a constant in human affairs; war was an aberration which could be avoided. They suggested that people have common interests in not fighting, and could discover this shared ideal. In the tradition of Woodrow Wilson, idealists believed that the proper form of national government would help prevent wars; democratic states gave the necessary voice to the publics who had no desire to make war, while totalitarian governments repressed the true wishes of their people. International organizations such as the League of Nations and the Permanent Court of International Justice could preserve peace, if they could be empowered to enforce international law. Balance of power policies no longer were valid or wise, since war had become too costly. The secret treaties and alliances that had led in part to the war were undemocratic, dangerous, and had to be ended. For the idealists, scholars had a role to play in the quest for global security; their (the scholars) job was to make these conclusions widely known both to average citizens and public officials, so as to help create the means for preserving peace.

Realists, by comparison, found little common ground with their competitors. War, the realists claimed, was not as rare as idealists believed, and while publics may not always want war, there have been enough wars for political, territorial, ethnic, economic, and religious reasons to suggest there are plenty of elements motivating nation-states to fight. Even democratic governments launch wars, the realists claimed, and since states cannot be expected to give to international organizations sufficient power to restrain sovereign countries, these agencies will generally remain impotent. As to the validity of balance of power tactics, the success of these assumptions in the nineteenth century shows that they have utility; in the case of the world war, they show that aggression should have been stopped sooner. And while the scholar could publicize his findings, the objective rules of human conduct were largely immutable.

This high-stakes intellectual battle raged throughout most of the interwar period, with both sides claiming to have a more accurate view of the subject, superior prescriptions for achieving general peace and tranquility, and preferable methods of studying the topic (Thompson, 1952:434-443). But by the late 1930s, world affairs seemed to be validating the realist interpretation. Naked territorial aggression in Europe, Africa, and Asia, and the seeming inability of the U.S. and European states, the League of Nations, and the PCIJ to respond, appeared to bolster realists' claims that force might only be stopped with counterposing force. E. H. Carr, in his seminal The Twenty Years' Crisis, 1919-1939 (1939) captured the tone of the debate in the period, when he indicted idealists for ignoring history's lessons and exaggerating policy makers' options, and castigated realists' reading of history as pessimistic and unimaginative. Yet even Carr seemed to side with the realists, despite their extremes as a group (Vasquez, 1983:16); given the situation at the close of the 1930s idealist prescriptions were simply too risky to adopt.

By the close of World War II realism as a body of thought was approaching the status of a "normal science" in paradigmatic terms. Idealism had been discredited, and the global political environment appeared to show the need for prudent policy making. It was in this time frame that Hans Morgenthau published what many consider today the earliest "exemplar" of realism as an integrated body of post-war thought (Vasquez, 1983:17).

In Politics Among Nations (1948[1973]) Morgenthau drew specific conclusions about the realist method of analyzing international politics, the shape of the subject under investigation, and the types of foreign policies dictated in such a world. As to the method of study, for example, realism assumed that nation-states (and their leaders) are the most vital actors on which to focus; this differed from idealists' concentration on individuals and international organizations. Realists saw a distinction between domestic and international politics. They saw the international sphere as more dangerous and anarchic than the domestic level, and objected to their opponents' claims that the external environment could be made to more resemble domestic affairs. International relations, realists argued, primarily focused on the search for power and peace--or more exactly, power to guarantee peace. Unlike many idealists, then, realists refused to deprecate the search for power as innately immoral; it was simply the natural way of conducting international transactions.

Morgenthau identified a number of features of "political realism" he found relevant to international politics (1948[1973:4-15]). First, politics, like society is ordered by permanent laws of human nature, which a scholar must recognize if he wishes to solve social ills. Second, "the main signpost" guiding realism in international politics is "the concept of interest defined in terms of power". Third, power is a "universally valid" category, although its meaning can change over time. Fourth, while "political realism is aware of the moral significance of political action", this does not negate the fifth principle, that "the moral aspirations of a particular nation" are not coequal with any general moral laws of human conduct. Finally, political realism, as a result of the other principles, is a "distinctive intellectual and moral attitude to matters political", and "the autonomy of the political sphere" is not to be denied.

The implications of these points for foreign policy making should be clear. According to Morgenthau, states are inevitably involved in trying to get, keep, and demonstrate power. The international system is indeed a self-help, anarchic complex of competing states. Cooperation among states is possible, and obviously desirable, but not inevitable; decision-makers would do well for themselves and their publics to remember that. Power should not be squandered, or used unwisely in unimportant areas or on trivial issues, because it is a useful tool.

An observer would be hard-pressed to summarize adequately the history of realist theory building in the last four decades. He would have similar difficulty relating the variety of "approaches", "frameworks", and "models" which deal with a broad assortment of topics that fit well within the realist camp. Nonetheless, he would be correct in saying that the fundamental assumptions underlying the realist paradigm can be recognized.[3] While there continues to be debate within different areas of research in realism, it is possible to delineate certain generally accepted tenets of realist theoretical discourse. A careful assessment of contemporary realist literature would reflect the following basic premises:

1) The international system is anarchic in nature.

The system lacks authoritative, supported enforcement structures. The structure of international politics is not one of chaos, but it is one of self-aggrandizing states. If order and security are present in the system, it is not usually the product of formal, freely arrived at agreements, but by some other factor; this is usually military hegemony, supported by political and economic capabilities. As states maneuver for position constantly, an ordered situation cannot be expected to endure.

2) The fundamental characteristic of the international system is the struggle for power.

All states recognize the anarchic nature of the system; they ignore it at their peril. Accordingly, they can be expected to seek advantages over other states, or at least a position of equilibrium. The most effective, dominant type of power is generally military; hence states arms themselves. The ability to prevail in a conflict is vital. Most systemic-level changes result from major wars such as the Napoleonic wars and the world wars, and from this governments believe they must be ready to have an impact in these struggles.

3) Nation-states are the most vital actors in the international system.

As the center of public allegiance and as keepers of military and economic capabilities, nation-states are most often the actors behind global political events. Actors internal to the nation-state are usually subservient to the national government; at very least the state can exert power over these sub-national actors. International organizations rarely subvert the will of the state, because these organizations are only given such power as states deem appropriate, and never enough to restrain sovereign state action. Accordingly, nation-states (and their leading officials) are the proper foci of study.

4) Political and security issues generally dominate all others.

The essence of the nation-state is at least partly its role in protecting its citizens. Therefore officials have a high moral calling which they may not abrogate. All other goals, such as civil freedoms and economic prosperity, only can be achieved if the nation-state is territorially secure. Other issues may dominate the policy agenda at times, but only when territorial and political security are assured.

5) <u>Patterns</u> <u>of</u> <u>political</u> <u>contact</u> <u>on</u> <u>the</u> <u>domestic</u> <u>level</u> <u>do</u> <u>not,</u> <u>and</u> <u>should</u> <u>not</u> <u>be</u> <u>expected</u> <u>to,</u> <u>repeat</u> <u>themselves</u> <u>on</u> <u>the</u> <u>international</u> <u>level</u>.

The domestic sphere of politics is ordered by shared cultural and socioeconomic values, and a police force exists to maintain order. The international area lacks all that; history shows the difficulty of creating such shared goals and enforcement structures on that level. It is dangerous for decision-makers to assume such ideas and structures will inevitably lead to peace.

Realism in Practice

While realism has been popular with scholars as a tool for studying and understanding the world, it also suggests policies to be followed. Hence it has been "home" for numerous American foreign policy makers since World War II (see for example Ambrose, 1988; Gaddis, 1982).

The previous section looked at the fundamentals of realism as a conceptual framework, as a set of understandings about global affairs. Before assessing how closely Reagan Administration policies approximated realist expectations, it is necessary to develop out of the above characteristics qualities of realism as policy. After doing so, it will be possible to estimate to what extent Administration actions were in step with the school of thought from which these officials claimed to be taking their cues.

With respect to the general characteristics of realist thought, a state whose decision-makers saw themselves in this tradition would likely act as follows:

1) <u>The</u> <u>international</u> <u>system</u> <u>is</u> <u>anarchic</u> <u>in</u> <u>nature</u>.

Seeing themselves as cautious, realist officials would assume the anarchy of the system. The nature of global politics dictates self-enforcement of international law, and the goals of one's foreign policy, since all other states can be expected to do the same. Because of the required suspicion of even friendly states, the realist will seek sound intelligence gathering capabilities. States must be willing to threaten the use of military force for important objectives, and to use that force.

2) <u>The</u> <u>fundamental</u> <u>characteristic</u> <u>of</u> <u>the</u> <u>international</u> <u>system</u> <u>is</u> <u>the</u> <u>struggle</u> <u>for</u> <u>power</u>.

In general the realist will pursue political, economic, and diplomatic advantages for his state, as officials in other states will be doing likewise. It is imperative to maintain an active military, capable of action against a variety of threats. The search for political and economic capabilities is continual, but the presumption is of the need to be able to fight armed conflicts, unless proven otherwise.

Because even allied states seek power, the assumption is toward the goal of being able to act unilaterally in as many situations as possible. "Multilateralism" should be reserved for action in policy areas where either the state cannot achieve goals by itself at an acceptable cost, or where the stakes are not so high as to risk a loss of prestige or capabilities by working in concert with other nation-states.

3) Nation-states are the most vital actors in the international system.

Nation-states are the most important forces behind global affairs, because they are assumed to control actors within domestic society, and because they do not give to international organizations sufficient power to enforce rules and decisions inimical to their will. Therefore the realist will be skeptical of the value of international organizations in pursuing state goals. Such parties can be expected to be self-aggrandizing, and almost certainly will become captives of smaller, more numerous states, whose voting power in such bodies is out of proportion with their real power. Such organizations are also suspect because they never need feel any sense of urgency about their security, as with territorial states, since these bodies are transnational in nature. Generally, diplomatic contacts will emphasize state actors.

4) Political and security issues generally dominate all others.

Realist officials can be expected to ask citizens to make sacrifices so that the nation's political and territorial security is insured; this may take the form of high military spending in relation to social causes. Security issues will remain at or near the top of the national policy agenda, and interest groups strategically placed to influence the agenda will gain in importance, further reinforcing the pattern of decision-making. The preservation of the nation-state, national values, and the established "way of life" will be seen as vital goals. Morality in foreign policy will be best served by defending those objectives.

5) Patterns of political contact on the domestic level do not, and should not be expected to, repeat themselves on the international level.

Because of the condition of the international system, it cannot be anticipated that the moral standards of domestic affairs will suffice in external relationships. The realist will be skeptical about chances of reforming the system, and will expect that certain actions which are indefensible domestically (such as espionage) may be required on the international level.

Both preceding lists of the qualities of realism--in theory and in practice--have intentionally been phrased in rather extreme forms. In the long run, such a view of the conditions of realism will help show its divergence from the conditions of complex interdependence, which Keohane and Nye say differ substantially from those of realism, but not always as obviously as systemic frameworks in other paradigms. More immediately, however, such a stark portrayal of realism provides a rigorous test of Reagan Administration policies. The more these "ideal" or near-ideal features of realist foreign policy are matched by Administration rhetoric and goals, the more absolute will be the distance between them and actual policies--and the more obvious will be the puzzle complex interdependence will try to explain.

Reagan and Realism

It may seem unnecessary to demonstrate that the Reagan Administration pursued realist objectives; for many observers this is intuitively accurate. But in theoretical terms there is a difference between a "hard-line" policy stance and intellectually informed realism. For instance, both liberals and conservatives in American politics have pursued hard-line goals in foreign policy, yet neither's position is necessarily explained as a result of their accepting realism as an integrated body of thought. Nor should the scholar make the mistakes of assuming that the statements of an individual indicate the mood of an entire Administration, and precisely forecast actions (see for example Anderson and Kernek, 1985). A careful appraisal of 1) the stated goals of Reagan and his officials, and 2) the early actions of the Administration, indicate both fit reasonably (albeit not perfectly) well within the realist policy framework set up in the previous section.

Stated Goals and Policies

The positions of Reagan and those close to him were no secret as the 1980 presidential campaign developed.[4] Reagan at the time was probably one of the better known American politicians, having been active in public speaking since before he lost the 1976 Republican nomination to Gerald Ford. When running for the presidency in 1980, his views were clearly hard-line and conservative. Cumings (1981:219) summarized Reagan's 1980 campaign this way:

In his VFW speech in August, Reagan referred to the Vietnam war as a "noble cause," to the Soviet buildup as the greatest "in the history of mankind", and remarked that "We're already in an arms race--but only the Soviets are racing". Two days later, in a Boston address to the American Legion, he referred to the Democrats

as "dominated...by the McGovernite wing", described the United
States as "second to one", and said the American people were sick
and tired of leadership that tells us "why we can't compete with
the Japanese and Germans, and...why we can't contain the Russians".
Earlier in another Chicago speech, Reagan had referred to the
ongoing battle with "Godless communism", and urged a
"housecleaning" of the State Department and a new "grand strategy"
for the 1980s. At other times, he called for funnelling weapons to
the rebels and blockading Cuba in response to the Afghanistan
invasion; he referred to the Shah of Iran as "as good an ally as
we've ever had"; called for assistance to free peoples in Central
America and deplored the Sandinista takeover in Nicaragua, and
argued for military superiority over the Soviet Union.

Reagan's policy pronouncements both during the campaign and in the
first months in office were in part derived from his staff of advisors;
most of these people were part of moderate-right to hardline institutes
and think tanks such as the American Enterprise Institute, the Hoover
Institution, the Heritage Foundation, and the Committee on the Present
Danger. Members of the last group included such highly placed personnel
as Richard Pipes, William Van Cleave, William Casey, Richard Allen, John
Connally, Eugene Rostow, and Fred Ikle (Cumings, 1981:220-221). Early
on, Reagan officials made clear the nature of the Administration's goals
and the preferred means of achieving them. Soon after taking office as
Secretary of State, Alexander M. Haig laid out the Reagan position in a
Washington, D.C. speech. U.S. actions, he said, were directed toward
three goals (1981:132):

> First, to enlarge our capacity to influence events and to make
> more effective use of the full range of our moral, political,
> scientific, economic, and military resources in the pursuit of our
> interests;

> Second, to convince our allies, friends, and adversaries--
> above all the Soviet Union--that America will act in a manner
> befitting our responsibilities as a trustee of freedom and peace;
> and

> Third, to offer hope and aid to the developing countries in
> their aspirations for a peaceful and prosperous future.

Haig stated the U.S. must "restore inflation-free economic growth" for
itself and the world, and "economic recovery must be accompanied by a
prompt correction of deficits in our military posture". These
accomplishments would allow the U.S. to pursue four broad aims:
restraining the Soviet Union, reinvigorating western alliances,
strengthening U.S. allies, and developing a more effective approach to
developing countries.

White House counselor Edwin Meese repeated the same basic themes, saying the Administration's objectives included "revamping the national economy, strengthening national defense, enhancing relationships with U.S. allies, improving relations with the Third World", and most importantly "dealing with the Soviet Union on 'a realistic basis'" (Kegley and Wittkopf, 1982:224). To achieve these goals, the U.S. would deemphasize human rights concerns in both allied states and LDCs, because such matters were internal affairs of no interest to the U.S. Also, the Administration would reaffirm the traditional Republican stress on free trade, and push for greater global reliance on market mechanisms for the creation of economic wealth and productivity. Developing states would be encouraged to be self-reliant, and not depend on the U.S. for assistance.

Through most of its first term, there is little to indicate that the Administration softened on its early goals. In September 1982, in a speech to the U.N. General Assembly, recently installed Secretary of State George Schultz said it was the Administration's intention to "start from realism" in the ways the U.S. understood and acted in world affairs. He indicated Soviet interference in Poland and Afghanistan, as well as its meddling in Third World states, was a strong indication of the Communist threat to western democracies and Japan. To respond to such challenges, Schultz maintained, the U.S. would have to "act from strength, both in power and purpose" (1982:8). In fact, "the bulwark of America's strength is military power for peace", he said, and the U.S. had the requisite "willingness to employ it [military force] in the cause of peace, justice, and security" (1982:11). A 'realistic' appraisal of global politics had lead the Administration to realize its duty to utilize American influence wherever needed in defense of freedom, Schultz claimed.

Administration Actions

Political rhetoric does not invariably equate to political action. Therefore, in addition to reviewing what some Administration officials said, to ascertain what the Reagan team wanted it is useful to review U.S. policies during the period in question. A comparison of policy actions expected from realists, with some of those actually taken by the Administration, reveals a fair correspondence between the two. Although official actions could be discussed in a variety of ways, for simplicity they are covered here in categories developed earlier in this chapter.

The international system is anarchic in nature. It was suggested that those who identify themselves as realists can be expected to claim a "realistic" awareness of the dangers of the international system, and would call for caution in dealing with potential or real opponents. They see the system as ungoverned, and assume competitors recognize this and act accordingly. International law is mainly useful only if states are willing to enforce it themselves; there is a need for effective intelligence gathering capabilities to ascertain threats and respond to them.

Reagan and his advisors acted largely as expected. They saw the Carter Administration as unwilling to see the international system as it was, with threats from the Soviet Union toward U.S. interests and those of its allies. The Carter Administration was portrayed as unable to cultivate an effective military structure, and to develop the will to use force. Reagan officials saw their predecessors as too concerned about the perception of America by LDCs who had nowhere else to turn for money, aid, and trade than the U.S. (Brown, 1983:594).

The Carter people, Reagan advisors felt, were unable to develop a coherent foreign policy, especially one the public would support. The Reagan Administration therefore "tried to end the ferment over foreign policy [in the U.S.] by reasserting" in some estimations "a classic Cold War outlook" (Hunt, 1987:1). In short order, and in response to its perceptions of the system, the Soviets, and the previous administration's frailties, the Reagan Administration devoted large sums of money toward the contra rebels fighting Nicaragua's Sandinista government. This policy eventually included Central Intelligence Agency participation in the mining of Nicaraguan harbors to prevent the importation of Soviet-supplied weapons that allegedly were then shipped to revolutionary forces in El Salvador. To contain Soviet influence in the region, the Administration sent advisors to assist the army of the U.S. backed El Salvadoran government, and aided that government with both military and economic assistance. In response to what the Administration saw as a serious weakening of the nation's intelligence community, it promised to 'unleash the CIA'. The Administration made clear its intention to respond to Soviet and Libyan efforts to train and supply terrorists for attacks on western interests.

The fundamental characteristic of the international system is the struggle for power. It was stated earlier that a realist will assume all other actors seek power, and that his nation-state must do so as well. Military force is the most dominant form of power, and the nation-state requires a strong capacity in this issue area, one that allows action on a variety of levels and in a range of locations. While the realist does not deny that power is also found in the political and economic spheres, he maintains that if the nation-state is threatened, military power will be the final option.

Reagan policies closely fit the model on this point. The military expansion the Administration designed is among the most well known of the Reagan initiatives. In terms of increasing the capabilities of American forces, which Reagan and his advisors believed were reduced during the previous decade, the U.S. spent unprecedented sums of money on all branches of the armed forces. This included spending on the B-1 bomber (resurrected after Carter cancelled it), the MX missile, and the Strategic Defense Initiative. Reagan pushed for a 600 ship navy with a global reach capacity, the stealth fighter and stealth bomber, and more troops. The buildup was accompanied by skepticism about arms control efforts. The Administration originally observed the terms of the unratified SALT II treaty, but then discarded the limits; it also slowed U.S. action on conventional force reduction talks in Europe. As to the actual use of force, the Administration was not reluctant to utilize American power; it committed troops in Lebanon for peacekeeping purposes, sent U.S. ships to the Persian Gulf to escort Kuwaiti oil tankers during the Iran-Iraq War, sent fighter aircraft to bomb suspected terrorist training camps in Libya, and launched an invasion of Grenada to oust the Marxist government there.

It was also suggested earlier that a realist would see it as unwise to depend on other states for assistance, even if these countries included long-standing allies. In other terms, unilateral capabilities would be a goal, even if multilateral action was willingly taken at times. The more independent the acting state had been in the past, the more reluctant it will be to coordinate its policies in the future.

The Reagan experience again bears this out. Early in the first term, Administration officials were notably unwilling to deal closely with other industrial powers about currency values and interest rates. This was partly due to their confidence in the efficiency of the free market, but also because they feared a loss of American policy flexibility in coordinated efforts. One especially clear example is the March 1981 decision of the Administration to halt seven years of negotiations on a multilateral Law of the Sea treaty; officials feared the possible impact on the private use of seabed resources and the loss of U.S. autonomy (Brown, 1983:600).

Nation-states are the most vital actors in the international system. It was suggested that realists are likely to see nation-states as the major causal forces in global affairs; they restrain the influences of subnational actors, and prevent international organizations from acting freely. As will be pointed out later, Reagan policy toward the IMF, the World Bank, and specific agencies of each reflected such a view. These bodies were seen as primarily mirroring the Third World goals of overturning the world trade and financial structure, and pursuing a New International Economic Order. Reagan officials saw the staffs of these organizations as not cognizant of the Soviet threat to global stability, and the need to place political security higher on the world policy agenda. Since these organizations were seen as possessing little power, the Administration generally put them low on its list of priorities, despite its objections to their goals. This was reflected in Reagan's original desire to miss the Cancun economic summit in October 1981. When the Administration did consent to discuss issues of development, it was essentially in forums where developed states predominated, such as the OECD, the GATT, and at the seven-nation annual summits of industrial powers.

Political and security issues generally dominate all others. Because of the inherent dangers of the international system, security issues will usually be of the utmost concern for the foreign policy realist. As would be expected, Reagan policies did exact sacrifices for its military expansion, in the form of reduced funds available for social programs. The Administration placed national security issues at or near the top of the policy agenda, and kept them there at least throughout its first term. More revealing, however, was the intentional deemphasis of various types of economic foreign aid and the discussion of North-South matters by the Administration. Well documented, for example, is the major shift in foreign aid from economic to military categories the Reagan approach directed.[5] Newfarmer (1983:41-42) reports that the 1981 fiscal year budget allotment of $3.3 billion in foreign military assistance was raised by the Administration by 91%, to $6.3 billion, in fiscal year 1984. Nonmilitary economic assistance in the same period rose only 21%; most of the increase was in Economic Support Funds devoted primarily to security purposes. Because of the Administration's "politicization of aid around nondevelopmental policy goals" a radical shift took place in the amount of aid going to states with the largest concentration of the "most poor": during the last three Carter years that amount was 63% of U.S. aid; in the 1981 through 1984 Reagan budgets that figure dropped to 43%. The Administration considered not meeting its quota for the International Development Agency (the "soft-loan" facility of the World Bank); Budget Director David Stockman and some Treasury officials wanted cutbacks on funding levels to which the U.S. had previously agreed (Rowen, 1985b:355). Only lobbying by Secretary of State Haig and U.N. Ambassador Jean Kirkpatrick saved most of those funds, because they were viewed as valuable for bilateral negotiating purposes (Newfarmer, 1983:35).

Patterns of political contact on the domestic level do not, and should not be expected to, repeat themselves on the international level. Because of the nature of the international system, and the policies which states must pursue, the relative civility expected in domestic affairs is rarely replicated in international dealings, according to our realist's expectations. The Reagan policies discussed above tend to reflect that assumption. "Conflicts and conquests, allies and enemies, and issues and interests" were "judged in relation to the overarching Soviet rivalry" (Harrison, 1981:6), which for the Administration was both the most obvious and salient indicator of a self-help world.

Conclusion

This chapter makes several points. It shows that realism is an integrated body of thought regarding the structure of, and processes which maintain, the international system. It also demonstrates that Reagan foreign policy goals and assumptions approximate reasonably well the realist model of foreign policy developed in this chapter. Of course, as the Administration progressed over time, especially into its second term, its adherence to these expectations varied; the divergence was most pronounced in its attitude toward the Soviet Union and arms control. But as was pointed out in the introduction, in managing international debt the Reagan presumptions and actions shifted early and dramatically from the realist norm. It is now time to review Keohane and Nye's rethinking of some of the elements of the realist tradition.

Endnotes

[1]For a review of the Napoleonic Wars, and the Concert system that followed, see Henry A. Kissinger, A World Restored: Metternich, Castlereagh, and the Problems of Peace, 1812-1822, Boston: Houghton Mifflin, 1957.

[2]The definitive statement on the workings of the classical balance of power system is Morton A. Kaplan, System and Process in International Politics, New York: Wiley, 1957.

[3]For a discussion of what constitutes a paradigm in international relations, see K.J. Holsti, The Dividing Discipline: Hegemony and Diversity in International Theory, Boston: Allen & Unwin, 1985.

[4]See, for example Lou Cannon, Reagan, New York: G.P. Putnam's Sons, 1982; Robert Dallek, Ronald Reagan: The Politics of Symbolism, London: Harvard University Press, 1984; Ronnie Dugger, On Reagan: The Man & His Presidency, New York: McGraw Hill, 1983; Thomas Ferguson and Joel Rogers, eds. The Hidden Election: Politics and Economics in the 1980 Presidential Election, New York: Pantheon Books, 1981.

[5]See Raymond Vernon and Debora L. Spar, Beyond Globalism: Remaking American Foreign Policy, New York: Free Press, 1989.

CHAPTER THREE

THE CHALLENGE OF COMPLEX INTERDEPENDENCE

As has been shown, realism continues to be popular as a body of ideas about the qualities of the international political system, and to a lesser extent about the structure of the international political economy. It has also been valuable as a description of how actors (usually nation-states) act to maintain that system. Partly as a result, realism provides policy prescriptions for decision makers; it furnishes an image of the world and suggests what states need to do to maintain their security.

Yet many theorists have been critical of the realist framework, the methods its advocates use to study their subject, and the implications of their findings. For example, critics see the assumption of systemic anarchy as incorrect, and argue that there is much more order and peace than realists recognize. Such observers believe the emphasis on military power leads states to look too readily toward armed conflict as a means of resolving disputes. It would be healthier, some suggest, to assume the typical country struggles for peace, not power. One often-voiced complaint is about the realist assumption of nation-states as the main actors in global affairs; opponents argue this ignores the influence of regimes, multinational corporations (MNCs), intergovernmental organizations (IGOs), and nongovernmental organizations (NGOs). Skeptics additionally question whether the focus on states seeking power omits investigation of other topics, such as social concerns over the environment, population growth, and human rights; these could be more important than military security, if war is or can be made less likely. Hoffman (1981:658) portrays this discussion as a debate between two groups. On one side are those he calls _modernes_, who point to "the importance of transnational and transgovernmental coalitions, of nonmilitary forms of power, and of multiple hierarchies depending upon the 'issue-area' or on the international regime". On the other side are their critics, realists who argue at the very least "that military power remains the _ultima ratio_, that the distribution of might remains the latent structure of the international system, and that the concern for survival and security remains the essence of foreign policy".

While much work to improve realism has been done by its supporters, others have worked in completely competing paradigms, which contest not merely the finer points of realism, but its fundamental conceptions about the shape of the international system and its workings. Included in this grouping are the approaches mentioned in Chapter One, specifically the dependency and global society paradigms. But also germane is the "functionalist" work of the 1940s and 1950s, which was based on the conviction that the creation of agencies to deal with specific problems common to a number of states could lead to the spillover effect of broader, peaceful cooperation.[1] Another example is the issue-based approach of Mansbach and Vasquez (1981), who deal with realism's faults by encouraging a focus more on issues than on states seeking power. More notable for present purposes is the 1971 special edition of International Organization which Keohane and Nye edited entitled "Transnational Relations and World Politics".[2] In it, Keohane and Nye emerged as influential observers and critics of orthodox realism (see Oliver, 1982). The text was a collection of articles on the increasing number and variety of actors and issues in world politics, especially of nonmilitary and nonsecurity natures. The volume deemphasized what Keohane and Nye called "easy to study yet frequently trivial aspects of international organization like roll-call voting in public international assemblies", and encouraged further study that entailed "first describing patterns of interaction in world politics and then asking what role international institutions do or should play" (1971:v).

Power and Interdependence

In the context of this debate in international relations, Power and Interdependence is unique, because unlike most other writers, in it Keohane and Nye specifically accept the utility of realism in some situations, and reject it and look for an alternative analytic framework in others. Power and Interdependence accordingly develops a sophisticated, situation- and issue-specific method of analyzing world politics and economics. As such, it may explain how policy makers could be both realists and nonrealists, at the same time and on different issues.

Keohane and Nye list two reasons for following their 1971 work with Power and Interdependence. In Transnational Relations and World Politics, they write, while they had "pointed out significant problems with realist theory, particularly in the area of international political economy", they had not developed an alternative approach. Also, "from a policy standpoint", they "thought that significant improvements in American policy on issues involving transnational relations and international organizations" were improbable unless the assumptions behind policy changed (1977:vii-viii). Theoretical and practical purposes motivate them, they say, to place "into a broader context" realist theory, because many dilemmas of U.S. foreign policy stem from the limits of realist thought, which seems sometimes incapable of explaining "the changing nature of the international system" (1977:viii).

Keohane and Nye are not content with the accuracy of realism as an approach to the international system, but they do not believe it should be completely discarded. Nor are they convinced some other approach to global affairs is inevitably preferable (1977:4):

> Neither the modernists nor the traditionalists have an adequate framework for understanding the politics of global interdependence. Modernists point correctly to the fundamental changes now taking place, but they often assume without sufficient analysis that advances in technology and increases in social and economic transactions will lead to a new world in which states, and their control of force, will no longer be important. Traditionalists are adept at showing flaws in the modernist vision by pointing out how military interdependence continues, but find it very difficult accurately to interpret today's multidimensional economic, social, and ecological interdependence.

In the 1960s many realist analysts did not recognize the rise of issues and actors that were not centered on security matters. The continued dominance of that approach in the late 1970s or 1980s would probably create even more seriously "unrealistic expectations", they write, but trading such an image for a similarly inaccurate view--for example, "that military force is obsolete and economic interdependence benign-- would condemn one to equally grave, though different, errors" (1977:5).

Therefore, the authors do not attempt to prove the superiority of either position; this would be "fruitless" because modern international politics involves both "continuity and change". Their task instead is to combine the benefits of both views, and to determine the <u>conditions in</u> which each interpretation will generate "accurate predictions and satisfactory explanations" (1977:4). In doing so Keohane and Nye hope to achieve two major objectives. The first involves determining the major features of world politics when interdependence, especially of an economic variety, is extensive. The second entails understanding how and why international regimes change (1977:5).

According to Keohane and Nye, international relations study has undergone significant changes in recent years. What they term "national security symbolism", which is supported by realist analysis, "not only epitomized a certain way of reacting to events, but helped to codify a perspective in which some changes, particularly those toward radical regimes in Third World countries, seemed inimical to national security, while fundamental changes in the economic relations among advanced industrialized countries seemed insignificant". But as the Cold War threat to security diminished in the early 1970s, "foreign economic competition and domestic distributional conflict" rose higher on national policy agendas in western industrial states, and the symbolic ability of "national security" considerations to justify alliances, foreign aid, and military involvements was similarly reduced, both for publics and scholars. The U.S. experience in Vietnam, and the rise of detente within the American diplomatic lexicon, both reflected such a shift as well (1977:6-7).

But the new rhetoric of interdependence, and the old rhetoric of national security, do not occupy much common ground (Keohane and Nye, 1977:7-8):

> In its extreme formulation, the former suggests that conflicts of interest are passé, whereas the latter argues that they are, and will remain, fundamental, and potentially violent. The confusion in knowing what analytical models to apply to world politics...is thus paralleled by confusion about the policies that should be employed by the United States. Neither interdependence rhetoric nor national security symbolism provides reliable guidelines for problems of extensive interdependence.

Adherents of the interdependence view, Keohane and Nye state, "often claim that since the survival of the human race is threatened by environmental as well as military dangers, conflicts of interest among states and peoples no longer exist" (1977:8). This conclusion could only be correct if three conditions obtained: 1) if there existed a threat to an international economic and ecological system on which "everyone" depended, 2) if all countries were at risk of such a disaster, and 3) if the existence of a single solution to this threat forced all actors to respond and share the costs involved. "Obviously", the authors write, "these conditions are rarely present". But if the interdependence framework overstates the case for economic and ecological interconnectedness, traditional approaches have their own problems. Security as conventionally understood "is not likely to be the principal issue facing governments" today, Keohane and Nye say. Because military power has little utility in certain situations, the usual definition of power is no longer adequate; what is required is the recognition that what constitutes power differs from one issue area to another. As for the concept of "national interest", it is becoming increasingly difficult to discuss effectively, because the linking of domestic and foreign policies have blurred the distinction between a nation's external and internal security. Subnational, governmental, and transnational actors have goals which often conflict; realist analysis does not account for these adequately (1977:8).

Throughout their introduction, Keohane and Nye carefully set the stage for the creation of a "left" version of realism, although they probably would not express it as such. They refuse to discard realism in total, nor do they embrace such a dramatically different view of the international system as can be found in global society or dependency models. In fact, their design of complex interdependence can be considered a "left" version of realism both methodologically and politically. In methodological terms, the authors' focus on an expanded set of issues and a variety of actors including (sometimes especially) nation-states makes their framework more flexible than orthodox realism, but without giving up on the value of studying traditional actors and their assumed concerns. Along a political dimension, the notion of complex interdependence suggests <u>some</u> of the more conventional ways of looking at the world, and hence acting in it, are outdated; nevertheless policy makers need not discard everything and begin searching for an alternative conceptual and policy map.

Since "power" and "interdependence" are two important terms in their text, Keohane and Nye spell out their exact understanding of those terms under complex interdependence. <u>Interdependence</u> simply means mutual dependence. They distinguish between "interconnectedness", in which "interactions do not have significant costly effects", and true interdependence, in which "there are reciprocal (although not necessarily symmetrical) costly effects of transactions" (1977:9). That is, for actors to be interdependent there must be a <u>shared</u> ability to impose <u>costs</u> on each other; there is no assumption of necessarily shared <u>benefits</u>. Keohane and Nye make clear that "The difference between traditional international politics and the politics of economic and ecological interdependence is <u>not</u> the difference between a world of 'zero-sum' (where one side's gain is the other side's loss) and 'nonzero-sum' games" (1977:10); <u>both</u> cooperation and competition can, and likely do, exist among interdependent actors, even in military affairs.

"Power" is also a vital concept for Keohane and Nye, and in addition to suggesting that within complex interdependence new resources make actors powerful, they also differentiate between two dimensions of power: <u>sensitivity</u> and <u>vulnerability</u>. Sensitivity refers to the likelihood of an actor suffering significant costs due to another's actions, <u>before</u> altering his policies to address the new situation. Vulnerability involves a target actor's "liability to suffer costs imposed by external events even after policies have been altered" (1977:13). Because varying policies quickly is difficult, the more immediate results of external policies usually reveal sensitivity dependence. Vulnerability dependence only becomes obvious over time, when the target actor has varied his policies in response to the changed environment.

An example of these two concepts would involve two countries which are both importing 35% of their oil. At first glance they would both seem equally sensitive to price increases, but "if one could shift to domestic sources at moderate cost, and the other had no such alternative, the second state would be more <u>vulnerable</u> than the first". Vulnerability, Keohane and Nye suggest, "rests on the relative availability and costliness of the alternatives that various actors face" (1977:13). Vulnerability interdependence includes a "strategic dimension"; this means that actors can use the greater danger experienced by other states to bolster their own position.

Keohane and Nye warn, however, that "manipulating economic or sociopolitical vulnerabilities...also bears risks" (1977:16), because efforts to manipulate an actor's dependence will likely engender countermeasures. And in the final analysis, military power will remain the ultimate option for a threatened actor, _even_ in situations of complex interdependence. "Military power", they write, "dominates economic power in the sense that economic means alone are likely to be ineffective against the serious use of military force"; this is the case even though the party taking action incurs greater costs for himself with military action. Therefore, even when an actor successfully manipulates asymmetrical interdependence in nonsecurity issue areas there is a chance of military retaliation, if the stakes are great enough.

The Characteristics of Complex Interdependence

According to Keohane and Nye, three assumptions are basic to realism (1977:22-24):

First, states as coherent units are the dominant actors in world politics. This is a double assumption: states are predominant; and they act as coherent units. Second, realists assume that force is a usable and effective instrument of policy. Other instruments may also be employed, but using or threatening force is the most effective means of wielding power. Third, partly because of their second assumption, realists assume a hierarchy of issues in world politics, headed by questions of military security: the "high politics" of military security dominates the "low politics" of economic and social affairs.

From their objections to these items they draw three characteristics of complex interdependence, each very loosely corresponding to the above features. These characteristics are those of the _structure_, that is, the distribution of capabilities, within the international system when realism is invalid (1977:22-29).

First, there are _multiple channels of contact_ among societies. They include both formal and informal ties among various levels of government and nongovernmental actors, and connections among transnational actors. These contacts fall into three categories. Interstate relations are the government-to-government ties emphasized in realism. Transgovernmental ties are those between different levels of government, often among bureaucracies that may act at cross-purposes to the goals of other state agencies. Transnational contacts are those among non-state actors, such as banks and multinational corporations, which may or may not act in harmony with the policies of their home state's government. With this expansion of the variety and number of international actors, state influence has necessarily been reduced, and the international agenda is more complex because issues which at one time were strictly domestic in nature are now intruding on the international level.

Second, the system is characterized by an absence of hierarchy among issues. Military security does not inevitably dominate the policy agenda. Domestic concerns now overlap into the external sphere, and the difference between the two is often unclear. Disparate government departments can be expected to hold different issues in highest regard, and consensus will be difficult to achieve, both as to which national goals are ascendant, and the means to achieve them. Keohane and Nye argue that different issues create diverse coalitions, both inside and across governments, and involve disparate amounts of conflict. In short, "politics does not stop at the waters' edge" (1977:25).

Third, in complex interdependence there is a minor role of military force. Among industrialized, western states the likelihood of conflict has diminished markedly. Moreover, given the two characteristics mentioned above, there are simply too many ties among interdependent states for force to be a useful method of settling disputes; that is, "employing force on one issue against an independent state with which one has a variety of relationships is likely to rupture mutually profitable relations on other issues" (1977:29). This is not to say the utility of force has completely disappeared. Given some "dramatic conflict or revolutionary change" one can imagine "the threat or use of military force over an economic issue or among advanced industrial countries" becoming possible. But in such a situation realist preconceptions would be more effective at providing an explanation (1977:28).

The Political Processes of Complex Interdependence

The three distinctive features of the international system just summarized produce distinct political processes by which actors achieve outcomes. According to Keohane and Nye, there are five[3] different political processes in complex interdependence (1977:114).

In terms of actor goals, in realist discourse military security will be the overriding concern for policy makers. Not only will nonmilitary issues be placed lower on the list of decision makers' priorities, but policies in other issue areas will often be scrutinized for their political and territorial implications. Keohane and Nye use the example of balance of payments issues being considered "at least as much in the light of their implications for world power generally as for their purely financial ramifications" (1977:30). But in the complex interdependence model, the expectation is that certain decision-makers, especially those within certain governmental agencies who have specific agendas, will have an assortment of objectives which they support. Without a "clear hierarchy of issues" goals will differ from one issue area to another, and there is no guarantee that military security will influence individuals' calculations. The situation is complicated by the existence of transnational actors who, on their own or through pressure on the state, press for nonsecurity priorities.

The linkage strategies used in complex interdependence will also differ from those found in realist situations. In the usual interpretation, since military capability is the dominant form of power, and power is fungible, the strongest state will be able to dictate or at least lead other states' policies in line with its own. As Keohane and Nye state, "Traditional analysis focuses on the international system, and leads us to anticipate similar political processes on a variety of issues" (1977:30). States with sizeable military and economic power will link their policies on some issues to those of other states on other issues. In complex interdependence, on the other hand, "congruence" between issue areas is less likely. With military force being downgraded in importance states will find it increasingly difficult to use their overall power to dictate outcomes in issue areas where their abilities are inadequate. Simply stated, the difference is between an interpretation in which states were either strong or weak, and one in which they can be both strong and weak, depending upon where one looks.

Because of the expansion in actors and issues, agenda formation has gained in importance. Traditional analysis placed little attention on the politics of agenda formation because policy concerns were assumed to be set by the international distribution of power. The "high politics" of military and political affairs dominated all other topics in orthodox realism. But as economic, ecological, and social concerns rise on the list of national and international priorities, decision makers must devote attention to new concerns, with once marginal actors involved.

Agenda formation is made more complex partly by the changes in transnational and transgovernmental relations. It is clear that there is an expanding number of actors involved in international affairs, with a growing set of concerns. Because so many of these actors are nongovernmental, it is increasingly difficult for governments to pursue policies in the "national interest" when there is no consensus as to what constitutes national interest. While realism assumes states act in their own interest, Keohane and Nye suggest complex interdependence asks two questions: "which self and which interest?" The situation is made even more complex when one realizes that not only are nongovernmental actors in conflict on issues, but within governments different bureaucracies can be in conflict, and these actors are cooperating and conflicting with each other across national boundaries. The result is that the pursuit of coherent policies is made more challenging. Keohane and Nye write that governments that are better equipped to maintain a coherent set of policies and philosophies will be more successful in manipulating situations of "uneven interdependence" than "fragmented states" that may appear to have more resources to apply on an issue (1977:35).

Finally, in complex interdependence international organizations can be expected to have an enhanced role in global affairs. In realist discourse such organizations are assumed to have marginal impact, because their concern with national security prevents states from conducting much meaningful business through such bodies. But in Keohane and Nye's interpretation, where multiple issues are imperfectly linked, and where coalitions in support of policies are created "transnationally and transgovernmentally," the role of international organizations in political negotiations will likely grow (1977:35). Such bodies help determine the international agenda, stimulate the formation of state and nonstate coalitions, and provide a locus for weak states to initiate political action and to link issues. More marginal actors, especially small and developing states, find these forums useful, because it is in these organizations that weaker actors can utilize their voting power, whereas their economic and military prowess is not as pronounced in other forums.

Models of Regime Change

The discussion in the previous two sections, on the characteristics and political processes of complex interdependence, deals with Keohane and Nye's attempt to answer their question about the conditions of world politics when complex interdependence exists. But they also want to know how the regimes which order international relations change, since their existence and functions can indicate whether realist or complex interdependence models are appropriate for explaining global politics. To that end, they utilize four different models of regime change, focusing on economic processes, the overall power structure within the system, the power structure within issue areas, and on power as utilized within international organizations.

The economic process model begins with the premise that Western economics does not have a theory of regime change, largely because it lacks a perspective on political affairs. Both political and economic elements are necessary, Keohane and Nye argue, for gaining explanatory insight into regime dynamics. Their model assumes that contemporary technical changes and increases in economic interdependence will make present international regimes obsolete, as inadequate to deal with the increased volume of transactions or novel types of organizations. Governments will be responsive to domestic political demands for a rising standard of living, as the dominant political goal within industrialized societies will be economic welfare. The major economic benefits resulting from the international movement of goods, capital, and (occasionally) labor will cause governments to "modify or reconstruct international regimes to restore their effectiveness". Regime transformation will be largely a matter of "adapting to new volumes and new forms of transnational economic activity. Governments will resist the temptation to disrupt or break regimes, because of the high costs to economic growth" (1977:40). Hence in the economic process

TABLE 2

**Political Processes Under Conditions of Realism
and Complex Interdependence**

Realism	Complex Interdependence
Goals of actors	
Military security will the dominant goal.	Goals of states will vary by issue be area. Transgovernmental politics will make goals difficult to define. Transnational actors will pursue their own goals.
Instruments of state policy	
Military force will be most effective, although economic and other instruments will also be used.	Power resources specific to issue areas will be most relevant. Manipulation of interdependence, international organizations, and transnational actors will be major instruments.
Agenda formation	
Potential shifts in the balance of power and security threats will set the agenda in high politics and will strongly influence other agendas.	Agenda will be affected by changes in the distribution of power resources within issue areas; the status of international regimes; changes in the importance of transnational actors; linkages from other issues and politicization as a result of rising sensitivity interdependence.
Linkage of issues	
Linkages will reduce differences in outcomes among issue areas and reinforce international hierarchy.	Linkages by strong states will be more difficult to make since force will be ineffective. Linkages by weak states through international organizations will erode rather than reinforce hierarchy.
Roles of international organizations	
Roles are minor, limited by state power and the importance of military force.	Organizations will set agendas, induce coalition-formation, and as arenas for political action by weak states. Ability to choose the organizational forum for an issue and to mobilize votes will be an important political resource.

Source: Keohane and Nye, 1977:37.

model, regimes will be "undermined from time to time by economic and technological change", yet they will not end completely; actors will adapt and reconstruct them in line with new demands.

In the overall power structure model (1977:42-48), Keohane and Nye's major emphasis is on the political and military power states possess within the international system. Military power is considered largely fungible, and therefore relevant for assessing the amount of influence states have not just with respect to security affairs, but in regards non-defense issue areas as well. This model's main appeal is its "simplicity" and its capacity for "parsimonious prediction". Assessments of military power seem easy to make, and it is taken for granted that it is possible to calculate supposedly rational policies based on those capabilities. The emphasis on state power and system structure in this model provides a traditional "realist" framework for studying and explaining regimes. The main dynamic force in the approach is the change in state power, which influences the distribution of power in the international system; changes in the rules of regimes result from that.

For realists, the type of leadership discussed in the overall structure model is most likely to take place in a hegemonic system, where one state is strong enough to establish, enforce, and terminate regime rules. Unfortunately for the hegemonic state, by setting up a generally peaceful international order, it creates the conditions in which other states can develop and eventually challenge for dominance.

The overall power structure model does not differentiate among issue areas. Instead it predicts a "congruence" among outcomes across issue areas because of power's fungibility. Keohane and Nye suggest that researchers should examine where the distribution of power between issue areas is uneven, because it is at these points that political struggle is likely to occur.

This approach is unable to provide a fully developed theory of regime change, according to Keohane and Nye. For instance, the simplest version of this model would see international economic regimes as directly reflecting changes in international political and military capabilities, assuming "high politics dominates low politics" (1977:46). But this falters as an explanation when one moves from explaining the general systemic structure to explaining change. A particularly apt example is that of the U.S.' loss of global economic domination while at the same time remaining militarily preeminent, or nearly so. Hence while military prowess affects the international economic power structure, it provides only part of the explanation. Keohane and Nye argue three necessary (albeit complicating) factors must be added to complete the model: (1) shifts in the assumptions about the likelihood of military threat; (2) changes in the comparative economic capabilities of the U.S. and its investment and trade associates; and (3) variations in the distribution of capabilities of Europe and Third World countries (1977:47).

The issue structure model of regime change challenges most of the assumptions of the previous model. Keohane and Nye point out that there are a variety of outcomes in economic matters that differ greatly from what would be expected if only military strength was important. The issue structure model "infers that linkages will not be drawn regularly and effectively among issue areas" (1977:50). Power in one issue area cannot be easily transferred to another issue area or transformed as such. In short, power is not fungible.

As in the the overall structure model, in the issue structure model strong states have the ultimate power in rule making. The basic assumption in the latter approach, however, is that while states may attempt to draw linkages among issues, they will usually be unsuccessful. As Keohane and Nye see it, the basis of issue structuralism is that the assets that make an actor powerful in one issue area may lose some or all of their utility in others. Hence, issue structuralism does not predict the congruence of power across a range of issue areas that overall structure explanation does (1977:50).

As an explanatory and predictive theory, the issue structure school is able to suggest "clear predictions for particular situations". Yet in general as a theory it has less power than does the overall structure model because more information is needed. Specifically, an analyst requires data on "not only the overall structure of military, or military and economic, power; but how that power is distributed by issue area" (Keohane and Nye, 1977:51). Issue structuralism allows analysts to predict that when sizable disparities exist between the distribution of capabilities in "the underlying structure, and its distribution in current use", regime change will be likely (1977:52).

As with the previous two models, the issue structure model does not offer a complete theory of regimes. Keohane and Nye point out that the model is useful when issues remain separated, but as linkages are formed between issues, the explanatory value of the model declines. This is so because the political results in specific issue areas will not be solely the result of power distributed in those areas, but in others as well. The issue structure approach, like the overall structure perspective, largely ignores power capabilities of anything but member nation-states. There is also likely to be a difference between power as a resource and as control over political and economic outcomes; this necessitates an understanding of both the structures and processes behind regime dynamics. Generally, however, Keohane and Nye reject neither the overall nor the issue structure models of regime change, because they remain the simplest starting points to discuss regime activities.

The last of Keohane and Nye's frameworks is the international organization model. Governments are linked through "intergovernmental and transgovernmental ties at many levels". These connections between governments can be either formal or informal; for Keohane and Nye "international organization" does not only refer to recognized structures, but also to "multilevel linkages, norms, and institutions. International organization in this sense is another type of world political structure" (1977:54). Over time, the capabilities of states will be of less use in predicting political and economic outcomes. Students of international organizations will need to recognize that "power over outcomes will be conferred by organizationally dependent capabilities" such as voting and the ability to build consensuses and coalitions (1977:55).

Keohane and Nye spend comparatively little time working out the intricacies of this model, at least in part because it is more complex than the previous three, and requires more information to work as a theory. The international organization model does not predict outcomes based on a single variable (for example, international structure). On the contrary, its focus on political processes related to organizations suggests actors have much to do with the forms regimes take, and their activities; in this sense it is much less deterministic than the structural frameworks.

Different models can be used to explain regime dynamics, Keohane and Nye suggest, depending upon existing international political and economic conditions. No one model is likely to be adequate for long periods of time. They argue that the closer a situation is to one of "complex interdependence", the more likely it is for the issue structure and international organization frameworks to explain and predict regime dynamics. Under realist conditions, it is more reasonable to expect the economic process and overall structure models to provide a perspective on regime rise, maintenance, and decline (1977:58). It is worth reiterating that at no time in their study do they do more than adjust the realist model of international politics; even in situations of complex interdependence Keohane and Nye believe realist assumptions capture many of the causal relationships in world affairs.

Conclusion

This chapter relates the theoretical and conceptual basics of Power and Interdependence, to indicate the complexity of the authors' alternative model to realism. The succeeding chapter reviews Keohane and Nye's use of the oceans space and resources and the monetary affairs issue areas to illustrate in concrete terms the difference between politics in situations of complex interdependence and realism. It will then be possible to show that the politics of international debt are better understood from a complex interdependence viewpoint.

Endnotes

[1]For an introduction to functionalist literature, see David Mitrany, "The Functional Approach to World Organization", International Affairs 24 (July 1948); also Charles Pentland, "Functionalism and Theories of International Political Integration", in A.J.R. Groom and Paul Taylor, eds. Theory and Practice in International Relations: Functionalism, New York: Crane, Russak, 1975.

[2]This text was later published as Transnational Relations and World Politics, Cambridge (MA): Harvard University Press, 1972.

[3]Keohane and Nye are not clear as to the exact nature of the political processes they isolate. In Chapter Two, Entitled "Realism and Complex Interdependence", they list five: actor goals, linkage strategies, agenda setting, transnational and transgovernmental relations, and roles of international organization. In their case study chapters "transnational and transgovernmental relations" is dropped and "instruments of state policy" is substituted. No explanation is given. Because this discrepancy seems to be minor, I have chosen to use the five original processes in this section; in discussing case studies later I will utilize the five Keohane and Nye focus on there.

CHAPTER FOUR

COMPLEX INTERDEPENDENCE IN OCEANS AND MONEY

This chapter and the one which follows are designed to assess the claim that the Reagan Administration found conditions of complex interdependence in the international debt issue area, and that it is possible to explain the puzzles of Reagan debt policies as stemming at least in part from the systemic constraints which existed. To do these tasks, it is necessary 1) to demonstrate that international debt was an issue area in which Keohane and Nye's model of complex interdependence more accurately conceptualizes affairs than does realism, and 2) to develop from that conclusion a set of characteristics expected in the foreign policy of nation-states in such situations.

This chapter reviews Keohane and Nye's demonstration of complex interdependence in the ocean space and resources and monetary affairs issue areas. This provides two test cases against which to compare the politics of international debt. Chapter Five first reviews international debt, using the framework Keohane and Nye utilize to cover their topics; evidence indicates that both the history and politics of debt as an issue area resemble the way with which oceans and money have been dealt. It then works from the politics and processes of complex interdependence as revealed in the three issue areas to suggest the policies expected of a state in complex interdependence. These propositions are then tested in the case study chapters.

Keohane and Nye choose oceans and money as issue areas because they have been vital topics since the nineteenth century; this allows them to test their approaches to complex interdependence "under changing political and economic conditions" (1977:63). While they make clear at the outset they do not believe any single model of regime change will be "superior" for the complete period under study, they do expect complex interdependence to apply more readily in recent decades than in earlier ones.

Historical Overview: Monetary Affairs

Keohane and Nye define the international monetary issue area as the group of issues seen by policy makers as pertinent to decisions about the design of international arrangements governing exchange rates, reserve assets, and the direction of international capital movements, and those issues related to "adjustment, liquidity, and confidence within a given regime or nonregime" (1977:66). This issue area only includes the major capitalist financial and trading states; specifically omitted are the Soviet Union, China, and other nation-states which are usually nonparticipants in large scale global monetary affairs.

Keohane and Nye focus on the history of international monetary regimes from 1920 to 1976. Regimes can be distinguished from each other by the rules and norms that restrict the freedom of the regime members, they say. It is relatively simple to note regime changes when the shifts in rules are obvious and dramatic, but when such changes are slow and piecemeal there may be no easy way to determine a break point between regimes. Nevertheless, the authors divide the five and one-half decades under investigation into seven different periods, including four "nonregime" and three "regime" eras.

The years from 1920 through 1925 Keohane and Nye term a nonregime situation. The conditions in the international political economy were inauspicious ones for all major actors. The desire of many states to return to a prewar gold standard led them to agree at Genoa in 1922 to reestablish a "gold exchange standard", which would allow currencies to be traded at fixed parities. Given then-current floating rates and competitive currency depreciations, many politicians believed the discipline imposed by the nineteenth century system of exchange was necessary to restore order in the global political economy.

The Genoa conference was important in that it presaged "the system that central bankers attempted to put into effect after Britain's return to gold in April 1925". This opened the international regime phase, in which Britain sought, at the urging of other states, to flex its economic muscle to bring some discipline to the monetary system. Britain was viewed by many as the key actor in the system, and its perceived power was such that the regime was established "by a series of unilateral actions, rather than by international conference or by systematic alignment of exchange rates on technical grounds" (1977:76). This arrangement Keohane and Nye identify as a "genuine regime", with recognized guidelines for action, open communication among central bank officials, and a high degree of cooperation, especially between th U.S. and British central banks. The problem was that the regime was politically and economically fragile, because of Britain's "diminished postwar position".

Keohane and Nye relate that when Britain left the gold standard in September 1931, it marked the beginning of another nonregime period of floating exchange rates, currency depreciations, and exchange controls. The U.S., which could have exerted some leadership in search of fundamental rules of international financial intercourse, was unwilling to do so. U.S. officials saw "no connection between war debts to the United States and reparations payments due its former allies" (1977:77);

this meant that war reparations were allowed to obstruct the search for a cooperative response to the international depression. When the U.S. went off the gold standard in April 1933, it did not consult with the British beforehand, and later that year Roosevelt's opposition to moves at the London Economic Conference to engineer exchange rate stability halted the meetings without any major accords. By 1936 there was "virtually no international cooperation", with major trading states competitively devaluing their currencies, and with currency values fluctuating violently. The Tripartite Monetary Agreement of 1936 between France, Britain, and the U.S. provided some short-lived hope of a creative solution to the problem of beggar-thy-neighbor policies; yet it "was not much more than a faint precursor of the international cooperation evidenced at Bretton Woods" (1977:77-78). During this period, cooperation was limited by economic nationalism, seen in the form of trade restrictions, exchange controls enforced by Germany, and an assortment of bilateral payments and exchange arrangements. Countries attempted to manipulate exchange rates for their own benefit, and freely floating currency values were rare. In a time of international economic depression and political turmoil, anything other than disarray in global monetary relations would have been very surprising.

In 1944 representatives from forty-four countries met at Bretton Woods to plan the structure of the post-World War II international monetary system. Keohane and Nye mark this as the establishment of a recovery regime which began operation in 1946. In contrast to the regime of the late 1920s, when central banks and private bankers had a great deal of influence, the goal of British and American officials at Bretton Woods was to create international institutions which would act on behalf of governments, not private financial actors. The fundamental feature of the new regime was that IMF member countries would establish and sustain "official par values for their currencies, which were to be changed only to correct a 'fundamental disequilibrium' in a country's balance of payments"; such action could only be taken in coordination with other member states. This would help insure currency convertibility. The IMF would assist states in maintaining their currency values, by lending them funds in accordance with a formula based on their subscription quotas to the Fund. The IMF itself was given substantial power, but its authority was limited in that voting within the organization was in accordance with the size of member states' quotas; this meant in practice the U.S. had veto capability. While the U.S. share of overall quotas has fallen since the Fund started operations, it still maintains a dominant voice in most IMF policies.

A transition period was provided for in the Bretton Woods agreements, during which member states need not adhere to all the requirements of the regime. This transition phase was left undefined, but evidence indicates it was not expected to last very long. In actuality, Keohane and Nye relate, the regular tenets of the Bretton Woods accords did not come into effect for twelve years. In December

1958 major European states formally adopted a convertibility scheme, and 1959 marked the start of a new international regime, one almost completely in line with the Bretton Woods expectations. This development was made possible economically because of the recovery of Europe and by U.S. balance of payments deficits which had pumped large amounts of dollars into Europe. Between the late 1950s and early 1960s world exports grew at seven percent per year, and American investment in foreign manufacturing rose markedly. In political terms, the turn of regimes was possible not just because of the hegemonic role of the U.S., but also because of "the development of networks of ties between central bankers as well as between treasuries" (1977:80). These included the development of the Bank for International Settlements and the Organization for European Economic Cooperation, which provided forums for European financial officials to coordinate policies.

Keohane and Nye suggest that the Bretton Woods regime, as is commonly recognized by now, did not always run smoothly. The established values for certain currencies proved difficult to maintain against foreign pressure. Not the least of its problems were runs on the pound, which forced the British to devalue it in 1967, and mounting pressure on the dollar throughout most of the 1960s. The system was fortunate in that "the institutional imagination and flexibility shown by the regime's managers contrasted sharply with the rigidity of currency values that member states sought to maintain" (1977:81).

One result of the massive American balance-of-payments deficits during the Bretton Woods regime was an accumulation of dollars in foreign hands. Moves by foreign interests to exchange their dollars for gold during the 1960s caused a precipitous decline in U.S. gold stocks; by 1971 there were far more dollars in foreign hands than the U.S. could possibly have redeemed in gold. In August 1971 the Nixon Administration announced a halt to the convertibility of the dollar, and devalued the currency. This marked the end of the Bretton Woods regime as it had been designed, and as it had functioned since 1959. According to Keohane and Nye, Nixon's action indicated the start of another nonregime period. The "elaborate but essentially ad hoc network of informal and institutional arrangements" (1977:83) which had sustained the system had been discarded.

What followed was a period of great uncertainty in the global political economy. It proved impossible to restore the convertibility of the dollar, and a variety of foreign exchange crises continued as they had before the break with the previous system. Both the dollar and the pound were devalued a number of times between late 1971 and early 1973. Values for the major trading currencies shifted dramatically for a time, and it was not until the middle of 1973 that decision-makers in finance ministries and central banks began to find favor with fluctuating exchange rates.

Keohane and Nye state that over time these officials began to accept that there might be benefits in not having to defend artificial exchange rates against speculation. Before long, "central banks began to intervene in the markets and to coordinate their interventions with one another"; after the 1973 oil price shock "it was often remarked that flexible rates had saved the international monetary system from a massive exchange rate crisis" (1977:83). Some observers suggested that with inflation at high levels, and varying from one state to another, flexible rates were imperative[1]. It was also suggested that it was impractical to expect politicians seeking public support and reelection to dispense with the use of exchange rates as policy tools.

Despite the growing attractiveness of flexible currency values, designing a regime around the incipient system was not simple. The process of constructing a new order started in September 1972 in the Committee on Reform on the International Monetary System and Related Issues, a body created by the IMF's Board of Governors. Originally constructed to reestablish "stable but adjustable rates", this task was proven impossible by events. Nonetheless, the Committee pushed reform in two areas. First, major countries acknowledged flexible rates were likely to remain the norm indefinitely, and adopted guidelines for floating exchange rates. Second, the Committee moved to reduce the role of gold in the international economy by giving special drawing rights (SDRs) a larger role in settling payments imbalances. In September 1974 the reform efforts became settled in an Interim Committee of the IMF's Board of Governors, with the U.S. and France as the major state actors, and a formal accord to amend the IMF's Articles of Agreement was reached in January 1976.

According to Keohane and Nye, this denotes the beginning of another international regime. The Interim Committee codified a number of features of the international monetary system which had become common practice, and decided on some new ones (1977:85)[2]. First, exchange values were allowed to float, under requirements that emphasized the expectation that member states would work with the IMF and other members to guarantee predictable and stable exchange rates. Governments were allowed to fix par values for their currencies, although this was no longer required. Fixed par values could be reestablished by a vote of Fund members possessing an eighty-five percent share of the organization's voting power. (This effectively gave the U.S. veto power.) Second, a variety of measures ensured that special drawing rights would be the main systemic reserve currency and the role of gold in the international monetary system would shrink. Third, the IMF was assigned the task of supervising the exchange rate policies of its members, under regulations it would develop later.

The Interim Committee also agreed to set up a trust fund for poor states; the fund would be built with proceeds from the sale of the IMF's gold reserves, and from voluntary member contributions. It also committed the Fund to establish credit facilities especially for LDCs.

Historical Overview: Oceans Space and Resources

Whereas monetary affairs have been high on the political agenda of western states for some time, oceans space and resources are a comparatively new concern at that level of importance. This, according to Keohane and Nye, is partly the result of technological changes that have increased the ability of humans to utilize increasing shares of the oceans for political and economic reasons. In fisheries, for example, the countries with major fishing fleets have increased in number, and new techniques have improved the efficiency of these fleets. Changes in merchant shipping have also been dramatic, with the world's total merchant tonnage increasing by more than three times between 1947 and 1974; the most obvious indicator may be the growth in oil tankers, both in their number and capacities. And while these traditional uses of oceans have increased, technological and economic shifts have produced new uses as well. The continental shelf area has developed into a major source of oil, and the possibility of mining the seabed for mineral resources has attracted much research and investment.

Keohane and Nye are primarily concerned with "the peacetime use and regulation of oceans space and resources". This oceans regime has two parts. The first deals with "the nature and extent of states' jurisdiction over the oceans adjoining their coasts", while the second covers "the ownership, use, and regulation of space and resources beyond national jurisdiction" (1977:89). This regime, then, has little to do with the use of the seas in wartime, but the actions states take within the regime often involve some thought to how they will affect nations' abilities to utilize naval power.

To understand the twentieth century oceans regimes, Keohane and Nye believe the observer must recognize the historical prevalence of the doctrine of freedom of the seas (1977:90-92). At least partly descended from the seventeenth century writings of Grotius, freedom of the seas is a long-standing doctrine which was often violated in reality, but only until Britain gained hegemonic status in the nineteenth century and was able to enforce the rules of the regime. Most state challengers to the regime then were small countries with limited coastlines and negligible fleets. When the tenets of the regime were violated, it was often during war; such violations had little to do with the shape of the regime in peacetime. Britain was especially careful to observe these precepts during peacetime, allowing other powers fishing and navigation rights near its islands.

Keohane and Nye find three regime periods in twentieth century oceans politics. Since the First World War, the doctrine of freedom of the seas declined from the status of a regime nearly universally adhered to by all important states (until 1945) "to a strong quasi regime in which most states adhered to the principle but strong challenges existed (1946-66)", to the present situation of "a weak quasi regime in which the challenges have become so great that the status of the rules is open to question (1967 to date)" (1977:92).

The structure of the free seas regime of 1920-1945 was largely unchallenged by major states. Britain's seapower after World War I, as measured by its proportion of world fleet tonnage, was even greater than before the conflict, and the second naval power, the U.S., substantially supported Britain and the regime. There were few attempts of any importance to overthrow the fundamental assumptions of the regime, Keohane and Nye say; a minor exception to regime rules was the American insistence on operating on the high seas to halt smuggling during Prohibition. The overall regime held up well, even in 1930 when a League of Nations conference at The Hague gave a number of marginal naval powers an opportunity to question the prevailing three-mile limit, and suggest a variety of other changes. The result nonetheless was that "twenty states representing 80 percent of shipping tonnage supported a three-mile territorial limit". Attempts by states to extend their control of coastal areas were usually unsuccessful during this period, and "even when disputes arose in such sub-issues as the antismuggling zones and fisheries arrangements between the United States and Japan in the 1930s, the disputing parties explicitly accepted the legitimacy of the overall regime" (1977:93).

The strong quasi regime of 1946-1966 was surprisingly given birth by the the U.S., which emerged from the Second World War as the leading naval power. Keohane and Nye point out the move from a free seas regime to a quasi free seas arrangement started with the Truman Declaration of 1945. Because of improvements in the technology of seabed oil exploration and fishing, "President Truman unilaterally established fishery conservation zones off the United States coast and asserted American jurisdiction over the adjacent underwater continental shelf 'appertaining to the United States' out to a depth of 200 meters" (1977:93). The U.S. phrased the language of its claims in general terms, in an attempt not to damage the regime basics, but a number of Latin American states saw the U.S. move as an opportunity to push their own claims to similar rights. Ecuador, Peru, and Chile maintained that their coastlines actually had very little coastal shelf to utilize, and instead claimed control as measured by distance from shore. The result was that the U.S.'s shift in position on shelf and fishing jurisdiction, which it could not sever from other issues, encouraged other states to make more extensive claims not in accord with the free seas doctrine.

This second twentieth century oceans regime, Keohane and Nye suggest, was "not fundamentally challenged, but there were signs of erosion caused by challenges in particular issues" (1977:94) Not surprisingly, the U.S. and Britain led attempts to protect the regime at UN conferences on the subject in Geneva in 1958 and 1960; one hallmark of these meetings was that there were twice as many states represented there than had been the case at The Hague conference, many expressing desires to adjust or discard parts of the regime. Attempts in Geneva to strengthen the quasi regime had limited success; while no state found it useful to dispute the freedom of seas doctrine directly, indirect attacks against the territorial seas jurisdictions were gradually becoming more telling. The East-West split in the regime, which was rather obvious through most of the postwar years, was by the early 1960s being replaced by the North-South dichotomy which would dominate in the next regime period.

The years since 1967 Keohane and Nye call one of a quasi weak regime, in which the freedom of the seas doctrine itself has been disputed. Its origin can be traced to a UN speech by Malta's ambassador Arvid Pardo, in which he discussed the possibilities of gaining wealth from the seabed and the importance of ocean resources. According to Keohane and Nye, Pardo's speech serves as a break point between regimes, in that since 1967 "the oceans have been treated less as a public highway from whose efficient management all states can gain", and more as an area in which "one state's gain is often seen as another state's loss" (1977:94).

Several shifts in regime politics separate the period since 1967 from the preceding era. One feature is a dramatic increase in the number of states taking part in regime affairs. Nearly 150 states entered discussions at the Law of the Sea Conference in 1976, an increase from 51 which had adhered to some part of the 1958 Geneva agreements. Various issues gained greater attention than before, including concerns about seabed resource mining and offshore oil drilling and tanker design. LDCs pushed for greater jurisdiction over coastal waters, or for some type of international regulatory agency, for fears that technically advanced and prosperous states would exploit ocean resources for their unilateral benefits. This prompted the UN General Assembly to designate the seabed as the "common heritage of mankind", and even induced states which during earlier regimes had been tied to major maritime powers to take a more individual view of their coastal resources. The shift in political and economic considerations was such that "even in the United States and Britain, important groups like oil companies and coastal fisherman gradually gained support for wide extension of jurisdiction" (Keohane and Nye, 1977:95).

The result of these shifts was that by the 1970s there had been a serious challenge to the doctrine of freedom of the seas. After 1967 "the situation...was not merely one of 'cheating on the regime', but of pressure for an alternative regime". Keohane and Nye conclude about this most recent ordering structure in oceans politics that in keeping with the prevailing "international philosophy of developmentalism", novel objectives such as "potential national wealth rather than tradition, defense, or general world welfare were asserted as the basis of rights in the use of oceans space and resources" (1977:95).

The Conditions of Complex Interdependence

Both realism and complex interdependence are conceptual ideal types for Keohane and Nye (1977:24). World politics can rarely be expected to fit perfectly within either category, but for their purposes, the oceans and money regimes both demonstrate characteristics of power distribution and political processes that are considerably closer to those of the complex interdependence model than the realist one.

The Role of Force

The conclusions to be drawn about force in the oceans regime are complex, Keohane and Nye argue. They admit that since the oceans are strategically important in foreign policy, force has played some role in the bargaining over oceans issues. The "dramatic change" worth noting, however, is the shift "from the use of force by great powers to reinforce a regime...to the use of force by small states to erode the established free seas regime by extending their jurisdiction". And even with the rise of small states willing to use measured amounts of military power to enforce their claims to larger coastal areas of control, many new issues have arisen which do not lend themselves to resolution by military means. The result is that (1977:103):

> The complexity of these patterns means that any general judgment about the role of force in oceans issues must be heavily qualified. Nevertheless, one can conclude that the actual situation in the oceans issue area lies somewhere between complex interdependence and realism: force is useful on particular questions, occasionally, but is not the predominant factor determining outcomes. In addition, force seems to be important on fewer ocean issues than it was before 1945, and on many conflicts it is not useable at all. Thus this condition of complex interdependence is approximated more closely for the oceans issue area since 1967 than earlier, particularly than before World War II.

The situation in monetary affairs has always more closely resembled complex interdependence than that in oceans, at least in the absence of the use or threat of force for monetary reasons. Keohane and Nye flatly state "There is no evidence...that governments during peacetime have ever threatened the direct use of force to change exchange rates, to induce other independent governments to hold particular currencies, or to secure support for preferred monetary regimes" (1977:103). This is not to say that there are no security considerations in monetary policies; clearly states have attempted to assess how monetary policies would influence their political and territorial positions, and they can be expected to try to harmonize the goals in the two areas. But usually, states try to pursue monetary policy goals with "policy instruments" that "come from within the issue area itself or from closely associated areas such as trade policy" (1977:104). Hence

Keohane and Nye conclude that on the subject of force, the politics of monetary affairs adhere more exactly to the complex interdependence model than the realist one, and that this situation had not changed in some time.

Absence of a Hierarchy of Issues

There has been no consistent hierarchy of issues in the oceans regime either, Keohane and Nye report. Security considerations were high on the list of Cold War actors during the second oceans regime, but of late different actors have entered the political debate and expanded the list of goals. In the U.S., for example, the navy's wishes for a free seas regime have often taken second place to economic interests in seabed wealth and concerns over pollution. This growing complexity of issues is reflected in the increased number of topics placed on the agenda at international conferences: at the Hague Conference in 1930 there were six major issues on the program; at the Caracas meetings in 1974 the list contained twenty-five major and almost one hundred minor issues.

In the field of monetary affairs, complex assortments of issues have also been the norm, but these "have generally been more tightly linked and have been very consistent over time" Keohane and Nye relate (1977:107). "On the whole", they report, "foreign policy agendas have been affected less by the proliferation of international monetary issues or by the loss of hierarchy among them than by variations in their salience over time" (1977:108). When monetary and related economic issues have been less contentious, matters of military security rise more easily to the top of national policy agendas; this makes a clear, but not necessarily accurate, hierarchy of issues appear. Keohane and Nye conclude that it is quite possible, even likely, that monetary affairs can rise to the status of "high politics"; in times of relatively widespread agreement about the features of the present monetary regime such affairs merely seem less vital (1977:109).

Multiple Channels of Contact

Both the oceans and monetary affairs issue areas have been characterized by multiple channels of contact, the authors report. In the 1920s, Keohane and Nye note, most of the ties between governments were bilateral in nature. Since then, the number of actors involved in bargaining has increased; this includes both more state and nonstate participants.

In oceans politics Keohane and Nye report a nearly four-fold increase in the number of international organizations active in the area, from five during the first regime period to nineteen as the third began. By 1975 that figure was nearly thirty if "regular conferences, interagency coordinating bodies, and minor fisheries commissions" were included. In the monetary affairs area the growth in the number of

TABLE 3

Changes in Complex Interdependence for Oceans and Money Issues, 1920s-1970s

Dimensions complex interdependence	How closely does the situation correspond to the complex interdependence model in the 1970s?	Have the patterns changed of over time toward the complex interdependence model?
Oceans		
Negligible role of force	Weak approximation to complex interdependence; role of force still not significant.	Yes, with qualifications: force now used <u>more</u> by weak nations, but force is not effective on many issues, especially for great powers.
Lack of hierarchy among issues.	Close approximation to complex interdependence; hierarchy difficult to maintain.	Yes.
Multiple channels of contact	Close approximation to complex interdependence.	Yes.
Money		
Negligible role of force	Fairly close approximation, although there are some linkages with force.	No. The role of force has always been minor and no clear trend is evident.
Lack of hierarchy among issues	Weak approximation to complex interdependence. Within the issue area issues remain quite closely linked and functionally related to one another; but when monetary issues are salient . . . the agenda is characterized by a less clear hierarchy of issues.	No. The pattern of close linkage among issues within the monetary area persists over time. Whenever monetary issues have become "high politics", the overall foreign policy hierarchy has been weakened--in 1933 as well as in 1971.

TABLE 3 - Continued.

Multiple channels of contact	Close approximation to complex interdependence.	Yes, but the pattern is not linear. Channels of contact were reduced in the early 1930s, but by the 1960s had reached unprecedented high levels.

Source: Keohane and Nye, 1977:113.

actual organizations has been less pronounced, but the variety of "communications networks among officials" had grown notably. By the beginning of the 1970s four IGOs were active in monetary affairs: the BIS, the IMF, the OECD, and the Monetary Committee of the EEC. Less formally recognized but just as vital was the Group of Ten. And because of the overlapping memberships of these bodies, "the elite network structure" involved in monetary negotiations had grown much more complex than could be understood from simply studying the politics of these organizations (1977:109-110).

Nongovernmental channels of contact have increased as well, if not in number at least in salience. Before the start of the second oceans regime, the main nonstate actors in oceans affairs were fishing interests and shipping firms. Since then, large oil and mining companies have become active, and so have a variety of groups with scientific, ecological, and political agendas. On the monetary front, while transnational actors such as American bankers have been important and obvious since the 1920s, their influence has fluctuated. After the start of the depression, "the importance of bankers...fell dramatically and transnational relations remained clearly subordinate to government policies for over a quarter century" (1977:111). It was not until three decades later, with the return of American banking interests to Europe and the growth of multinational corporations, that transnational actors regained large-scale influence in the global economy. Since that period, monetary politics, like oceans affairs, "shows a clear trend toward the increased importance of large, sophisticated organizations in transnational activity" (1977:111).

Table Three summarizes Keohane and Nye's discussion of the characteristics of complex interdependence in oceans and money. In the 1970s, they write, while neither one conforms exactly with an ideal type of complex interdependence, the distribution of capabilities in both areas more closely resembles their model than a realist one.

The Political Process in Money and Oceans

Realist models of world politics assume a number of constraints on foreign policy makers, Keohane and Nye suggest. The assumptions decision makers must make about the self-help nature of the international system reduce the variety of options they have in initiating policies or responding to those of others. The presumptions inherent in complex interdependence mitigate some of these constraints, the authors argue; for instance, "the emergence of multiple channels of contact between countries, on multiple and nonhierarchic issues, increases the opportunities for influence" (1977:112). But there is a down side to this fact, they caution. Multiple channels of contact, for example, can provide increased opportunities for governments to exert their influence, but give other actors chances to influence state policies. These channels of contact also imply an assortment of transnational contacts, which can adversely affect governments' efforts to pursue coherent policies.

As they do in the theoretical chapters of their text, Keohane and Nye posit five aspects of the political process which can be expected to differ in complex interdependence from their workings in realist conditions. The first has to do with actor goals. From the assumptions of complex interdependence, they deduce three propositions. The first is that the goals of states will vary by issue area. On one level, they say, this is obvious; the history of politics in oceans and money bear out that national objectives cannot always be consistent across policy areas. But underlying is the question of whether military goals supersede all others. Again, the history of their two test cases supports their framework; in the oceans area military and security considerations have increasingly taken second place to political, economic, and ecological concerns, not only for small states but for major maritime powers too. In monetary matters, as they illustrate, "security goals have periodically been relevant, but they have not been determining" (1977:115). Their second proposition about actor goals is that transnational actors can be expected to pursue goals which vary by issue area; this is virtually true by definition.

Keohane and Nye's third proposition is the one they find the most important: "transgovernmental politics will make it difficult for states to pursue clearly specified goals" (1977:115). In their estimation, the affairs in their test regimes indicate such a proposition must be modified, in that "under some circumstances--when domestic interests are sharply divided, issues are diverse, and the attention of top political leaders is not focused on the issues--transgovernmental coalitions can make state goals difficult to define". On the other hand, "when domestic interests are fairly consistent and the top political leaders highly concerned about the issues, governments still may pursue coherent policy goals, even under conditions of complex interdependence" (1977:118-119). In short, the search for policy coherence is made more difficult under complex interdependence, but it is not impossible to achieve.

The second political process Keohane and Nye review are the instruments of policy states utilize. Under realist assumptions, force is the ultimate means of achieving goals, but in their alternative formulation of global politics the manipulation of interdependence, international organizations, and transnational actors can be more useful. Such has been the situation in the oceans regime, the authors believe; the perceived utility of force has declined over succeeding regime periods, and once marginal states have become more capable of maneuvering for advantages in new forums. When major powers found themselves facing the downfall of more preferable regimes, they attempted to use the forums of international organizations to convince LDCs of the utility of the previous ways of conducting business; these powers could not contemplate utilizing military means for the goals at hand. And in monetary issues the result has been the same. Force, Keohane and Nye maintain, has not been used or threatened in pursuit of monetary policies; its only connection to the money regime has been when the U.S. has attempted to link defense issues to money issues in discussions with its allies.

Closely related is the third process, that of agenda formation. Realism predicts the agenda in an issue area will be set by the overall distribution of power. Complex interdependence, Keohane and Nye write, sees the political agenda as influenced mainly by shifts in the distributions of capabilities within the issue area, as well as by a range of processes including "the evolution of international regimes, and their ability to cope with changing economic and technological circumstances; changes in the importance of transnational actors; linkages from other issues; and politicization as a result of domestic politics" (1977:121).

The political changes in the oceans and money regimes fit these characteristics of complex interdependence rather closely. The agenda in monetary affairs, the authors say, has generally been conditioned by the difficulties in constructing and preserving the regime amidst myriad external pressures. In like fashion, the oceans regimes have been effected by the technological and economic variations which have presented changing opportunities and threats to various actors. In both these areas, Keohane and Nye conclude the expectation that "security threats will not be a major source of agenda change" (1977:122) is borne out. But they caution that it will be difficult to understand how changes in policy agendas are made, because of the variety of factors involved.

Much as is the case in agenda setting, in the fourth process, issue linkage, the realist position assumes issues will be linked most successfully by strong nation-states, because of the fungibility of their power. The complex interdependence model, however, assumes that since power in one issue area is not necessarily useful in another area, that strong states cannot be expected to be uniformly capable across disparate policy areas. This indicates that when issues are linked they may be done so quite often by weaker states operating in international organizations.

This has indeed been the case in oceans politics in recent years, Keohane and Nye state. A review of the history of oceans conferences reveals a number of instances in which small states managed to link issues, often because of the voting strength which the larger but less numerous maritime powers do not possess. In monetary affairs the processes involved in linking issues has been different, but the linkages are more vital. First, because of the close political and economic relationships between exchange rates, convertibility issues, and macroeconomic policy, the fact that states have linked policies on money to other financial topics is not surprising. Second, powerful nation-states, in addition to weak ones, have been able to link issues in monetary affairs. This is at least partly because of their concomitant capabilities in other economic issue areas, and because their financial resources translate more readily into votes in international organizations. Small states have less to bargain with in monetary issues, Keohane and Nye point out; "on oceans, they could always make trouble by declaring extended jurisdiction and harassing anyone who violated their newly declared area of control; on monetary issues, their only weapon was the costly one of default" (1977:124).

Given what has been said previously, it is nearly superfluous to indicate Keohane and Nye's fifth conclusion, that the role of international organizations has become greater when world politics approximates conditions of complex interdependence. In the oceans issue area, for example, international organizations have grown in number in the last few years, and more importantly "the politics of rule-making in the oceans issue area has become closely associated with international organizations". These organizations "have politicized oceans issues and have greatly increased the number of states active in these questions" (1977:124-125), and placed the dominant maritime states on the defensive in Law of the Sea negotiations.

In monetary affairs there has been no corresponding rise in the number of influential international organizations. This is because such actors as the BIS, the IMF, the OECD, and others have been in existence for some time, and have provided a place in which transnational communications have taken place. Attempts by LDCs to enter the discussions in these forums have met with limited success, Keohane and Nye write; there has not been the "explosive growth of Third World participation and influence" in monetary affairs as there has been in oceans negotiations. Unlike the situation in the oceans area, they say, in the monetary affairs structure membership in the policy making elite has been set for some time, and is difficult to enter.

Keohane and Nye conclude that in the first half of the 1970s in both issue areas they isolate the processes are closer to the expectations of complex interdependence than realism, but the congruity was much greater for oceans than money. LDCs, for example, had more impact in the oceans area, and were more important actors in international organizations (1977:126).

Endnotes

[1]Their source is Marina V. N. Whitman, "The Payments Adjustment Process and the Exchange Rate Regime: What Have We Learned?" <u>American</u> <u>Economic</u> <u>Review</u>, May 1975, p. 144.

[2]Taken from <u>IMF</u> <u>Survey</u>, January 19, 1976.

CHAPTER FIVE

COMPLEX INTERDEPENDENCE IN INTERNATIONAL DEBT

While Keohane and Nye study the politics of the oceans and money regimes over periods longer than five decades, international debt as an issue area has a considerably shorter history. Unless a student wishes to expand his study to the broader topics of "international economics" or "international finance", an adequate summary of the current debt "crisis" and its causes can be obtained by studying events of the last two decades. In fact, Kahler (1986b:26) reports that the "existence of a coherent regime" in debt management is doubtful before late 1982. Prior to that, he says, some general "case law" existed on the subject of sovereign debt, "but to posit an existing regime is to understate the level of innovation" in multilateral debt management after Mexico's near default.

The comparative novelty of international debt need not be a serious impediment to its study from a complex interdependence standpoint. As this chapter will indicate, it is still possible to assess the characteristics and processes of politics in conditions of complex interdependence. It will not, however, be possible to test completely the validity of the different models of regime change (see Chapter Three) which Keohane and Nye apply to oceans and money.

This situation will perhaps weaken the attempt to apply an alternative framework to the issue area of international debt. Most of this section involves an attempt to address Keohane and Nye's first question: what are the characteristics of world politics when complex interdependence exists? It cannot deal very convincingly with their second question: how and why do international regimes change? Some questions may therefore arise for which no definitive answer can be given; one would be about the possibility that the recent politics involved in international debt reflect idiosyncratic factors not likely to exist for long in the issue area. The inclusion of Reagan debt policies in this study consequently may strengthen the argument.

Historical Overview: International Debt

Early Lending

The history of interstate finance is a lengthy one. Various forms of cross-border lending have existed almost since the establishment of the modern state system (Makin, 1984:37-38); this includes state to state lending, and private lending to other private interests and states. Not surprisingly, therefore, the history of state and private defaults or near-defaults with international repercussions is long also (Kettell and Magnus, 1986:29-36). Notable defaults on externally held obligations occurred in Europe in the early 1800s, and again after the depression of the 1930s; Russia repudiated the debts of the Czarist government after the revolution. Even some U.S. states refused to recognize debts incurred by former territorial governments (Makin, 1984:40-43).

But in comparison with today's debt levels, these debt payment problems were narrow in the size of the loans at stake, the number of participants, and the potential and realized effects on the international economy. As the international debt situation stands at the start of the 1990s, far larger sums, both in nominal and real terms, are involved than most observers in the 1970s and early 1980s would have anticipated. The same is true for the number of lenders and borrowers. And the importance of debt may be greater than ever before, especially as measured in social costs: much of the financial obligations incurred by LDCs has gone into badly needed development projects which Third World governments are reluctant to scale back.

In short, revolutions in the "magnitude and locus" of international lending have taken place. In past times money was loaned primarily by states, which could protect themselves against losses, but by 1983 the "world's commercial banks owned more than half of the over $700 billion or so owed by developing countries" (Makin,1984:19). And whereas before this recent explosion in international lending money was sent to specific industries and economic sectors, now much of it is lent to state governments which decide how the funds will be used. From what used to be a bilateral matter between lending and borrowing states, the international system has witnessed the rise of debt as a multilateral issue, with widespread implications.

The Rise in External Debt

The growth in the external debt market, both in the amount of funds lent and the number of participants, is largely a product of forces of the last two decades. A look at some of these factors helps to draw comparisons between the forces involved in debt management and those active in the oceans and money regimes. This discussion does not attempt to rank these forces and actors in order of importance; instead it is structured loosely along historical lines.

A good place to start to explain the rise in Third World debt levels is with the development of the "Eurodollar" markets in the last two decades.[1] This refers to the existence of large amounts of American dollars held in banks outside the U.S., often in Europe (hence the name). Being outside the jurisdiction of any single state gives these banks the ability to avoid the financial regulations of various state governments, and their separate branches translates into widely spread power in gaining deposits and lending funds. The rise of these markets has allowed a tremendous expansion of international lending, Makin writes (1984:23); he says the rise of these structures, especially with the concomitant growth of interbank lending, has helped to integrate the world's financial system.[2] Stallings (1987:89-91) says the growth of the Eurocurrency system was one of the two major causes of the growth of lending to Latin America, and the expansion in the role of international "money center" banks there in the 1970s. This was because these banks attracted funds with high interest rates on deposits and lent money at lower interest rates (at the time) than competing domestic banks. These firms also helped cause the second major reason for expanded lending in the area, according to Stallings, which was the growth of branch banking.

Accompanying and partly caused by the rise of international banking was a shift in the nature of international lending, and hence on the degree of emphasis placed on lending for profit. Prior to 1970, most international loans were made by governments and international agencies, at fixed interest rates, and at long maturities. In the 1970s, especially in the second half of the decade, the majority of lending was increasingly being done by large money center banks headquartered in the U.S., Japan, or Western Europe (Sjaastad, 1983:305). Stated more broadly, private lending had outstripped public lending. In the 1960s, non-OPEC LDCs got 50% of their net external resources on concessional terms; between 1974 and 1979 official export credits and development aid declined to less than one-third of external financing. Fully 60% of total external funding was now coming from commercial banks (Lipson, 1981:611). The shift in funding and its impact were clear, and perhaps most obvious in Latin America in the 1970s. Frieden, writing at the close of the decade, said that "private financial institutions have displaced multilateral corporations and official aid" over the previous fifteen years as the most vital source of foreign funding for the region (1981:407). Stallings (1987:148-149) reports that U.S. banks were especially willing to increase their foreign lending in this period, with the advent of three changes in the way loans were made. The first was the development of syndication, which strengthened the positions of smaller banks and limited their risks; the second was the beginning of floating interest rates, which banks saw as protecting them against inflation; the third was the creation of cross default clauses in loan agreements, which prevented debtors from using banks against each other.

The result of these transformations was to make international lending more profitable and structured.

If the global oil price "shock" of 1973-1974 was fortuitous for anyone other than oil producers, it was international banks, which had to decide what to do with the huge influx of "petrodollars" OPEC states were depositing in their accounts. The oil "crisis" occurred as a number of other factors made their impact on international lending. Borrowers, lenders, and banks had by then learned to utilize and like the Eurocurrency system; important before the 1973 embargo, banks used the turn of events and price rises to grow even more important (Lipson, 1981:604). The debt levels of LDCs began to mount dramatically. Oil-led inflation and recession in developed states reduced LDC exports to them, and raised the prices of Third World imports (Frieden, 1981:409). OPEC petrodollar surpluses in western banks and prevailing inflation rates kept the real rates of interest low on "dollar-denominated external debt" (Sjaastad, 1983:309); this provided an incentive for developing states to borrow. Indeed, it was said by some at the time that given the real interest rates available, LDCs could hardly have too much debt.

Perhaps not surprisingly, international banks were happy to oblige. As has been documented, banks found lending hundreds of millions of dollars as easy as lending a few million dollars, just as safe--because of the assumption that 'sovereign states don't default'--and "much more profitable" (Makin, 1984:7). Some banks became "debt pushers" (Darity and Horn, 1988), competing with other banks for profits and lending larger sums. The result was, according to World Bank data, that in 1970 LDCs owed $63.9 billion to foreign creditors, but by the end of 1978 that figure had grown to $313.5 billion (Frieden, 1981:409). For developing states which faced the unpopular step of cutting back development programs if new loans were not forthcoming, the choices were few--and obvious.

Throughout this boom period, primarily the 1970s, warning signs about the dangers of mounting debt totals and the risk of potential debt service difficulties were ignored for the most part. Bankers, clearly too ignorant of history, assumed that sovereign states could not or would not abrogate their financial responsibilities. But this was only one of a number of fallacies to which they adhered. Kettell and Magnus (1986:61-69) identify four other notable ones. The "oil-in-the-ground fallacy" assumed that debtor states usually had a sufficient reserve of mineral wealth available to pay their debts. The "short-term lending fallacy" presumed that a rapid rise in quickly maturing loans was not an indication of a state's lack of financial stability. The "austerity fallacy" assumed that austerity programs would inevitably return to economic prosperity any LDC facing financial problems. The most subscribed-to illusion was probably the "umbrella fallacy", which imputed to certain states the capacity to compel debt payments from LDCs supposedly under their control. This was the purported situation with

U.S. power over Iran under the Shah, and over Latin America; the Soviet Union was said by some to have umbrella responsibility for Eastern Europe. By the close of the 1970s, the results of the changes in the decade's lending and borrowing patterns were clear to those who looked (although in retrospect not enough people did). For American banks, in June 1979 the nine largest banks had loaned 113% of their reserve capital to only six countries: Argentina, Brazil, Mexico, the Philippines, South Korea, and Taiwan. The amount at stake in Brazil alone equaled one-half of "all U.S. bank capital" at risk (Lipson, 1981:614). For the LDCs, the figures were equally stark: in 1970 the

TABLE 4

INCIDENCE OF EXTERNAL DEBT RESCHEDULINGS, 1972-1982

Year	Country	Debt	
		billions of dollars[a]	percentage of total[b]
1972	Chile	3.3	4.3
1973	----	---	---
1974	Chile	4.4	3.4
1975	Chile	4.7	3.0
1976	Argentina Peru Zaire	15.9	8.5
1977	Zaire	2.9	1.2
1978	Peru Turkey	15.9	5.4
1979	Turkey Peru Sudan Zaire	27.3	7.9
1980	Turkey Zaire	18.8	4.2
1981	Bolivia Sudan Zaire	12.0	2.3

TABLE 4 - Continued

1982	Argentina	242.3	40.4
	Brazil		
	Mexico		
	Turkey		
	Romania		
	Sudan		

Source: Cline, 1984:236.

aRefers to total country debt, not rescheduled amount.

bTotal is for thirty-one large debt countries.

twelve largest non-oil producing LDCs owed $1.1 billion in interest on their external debt (equivalent to 6% of their export earnings); in 1980 the amount was $18.4 billion (equivalent to 14% of their export earnings) (Lipson, 1981:603).

Warning Signs

Well before the debt "crisis" was recognized in the popular press in late 1982, there were indications of the mutual dependence of creditor and debtor states, MDBs, and banks.

One example of this interdependence is the rising incidence of debt service problems experienced by LDCs. External debt reschedulings rose dramatically in the 1970s, both in number and in the amount of money involved. As Table Four indicates, in the decade from 1972 until the debt crisis broke in 1982, debt payment reschedulings increased from a relatively small number, involving a very small portion of total LDC external debt, to encompass over 40% of the total external debt held by the thirty-one largest debtors.

In addition to indications states were having difficulties paying debt obligations, warning signs suggested future trouble because of the way LDCs were obtaining credit. According to Kuczynski (1988:79-80), in 1979 and 1980 there was a rapid rise in the amount of short-term financing being arranged by developing countries. Debtors which had before--in boom years for borrowing--desired and been eligible for longer term loans at attractive interest rates now were being forced to take more costly short maturity loans, because of the reluctance of major banks to extend long-term credit. As Kuczynski makes clear, short-term borrowing has its purposes, but the shift here was an indication that banks had changed their thinking about how attractive LDCs were as targets for loans. This shift in lending only compounded

TABLE 5

AVERAGE SPREAD OVER LIBOR EUROCREDITS, 1975-1980

	Average Margins (Percent over LIBOR)		Ranges[a] (Percent over LIBOR)	
	Industrial Countries	Developing Countries	Industrial Countries	Developing Countries
1975	1.39	1.59	1.00-1.75	1.25-2.00
1976	1.36	1.62	1.00-1.75	1.00-2.25
1977	0.96	1.42	0.50-1.50	0.75-2.00
1978	0.60	1.10	0.25-1.25	0.50-2.00
1979	0.48	0.78	0.25-1.00	0.25-1.50
1980[b]	0.44	0.74	0.25-0.75	0.25-1.50
1980[c]	0.42	0.85	0.25-0.75	0.25-1.50

Source: Richard Bernal, "Transnational Banks, the International Monetary Fund and External Debt of Developing Countries," Social and Economic Studies 31 (1982):75. Cited in Darity and Horn, 1988:178.

[a]Excludes top and bottom ten percent of distribution.

[b]First half of year.

[c]Second half of year.

the danger of financial problems for debtors, because of the greater chance of a credit "squeeze" if short-term loans were not renewed. In 1979, for example, in Latin America short term debt was 16% of total external debt, and 43% of export earnings for the year. In 1981 the total had risen to 43% and 70%, respectively.

These shifts were also reflected in the prevailing interest rates LDCs had to pay for loans. The data in Table Five indicate that in the late 1970s LDCs could still obtain loans at competitive interest rates, especially in comparison with the rates offered them in the middle of the decade. But overall their rates were on the rise, while those offered to developed states were declining. The result of course was a reduction in funds these states could devote toward local projects,

TABLE 6

INTEREST RATES AND EXTERNAL BORROWING FROM BANKS, 1978-1982
(In billions of U.S. dollars)

	1978	1979	1980	1981		Cumulative Total
1. Actual interest paid to banks	9	15	22	32	30	108
2. Actual interest rate paid to banks (percentage)	10.0	13.4	15.4	18.0	14.8	
3. Amount which would have been paid at 10%	9	12	15	18	21	75
4. Difference between 1 and 3 plus compounding at current interest rate = borrowing due to interest above 10%	--	4	9	17	14	44

Source: Bank of International Settlements data. Cited in Kuczynski, 1988:82.

especially of an investment nature, which in the medium and short term could have bolstered their debt service and export positions. (See also Table Six).

By the end of the 1970s, the debt boom was nearly over, and several money center banks had begun to express their concern over the ability of LDCs to service their debt, let alone pay off the principal (Crittenden, 1980). However LDC debt was expressed, 1980 and 1981 were years of substantial, rapid deterioration in the credit standing of most debtor countries (see Figure Two). The situation was merely worsened by the realization of some banks of just how exposed (or overexposed) they were. (See Table Seven).

The Music Stops

A number of events and factors combined in the early 1980s to make an already unfortunate situation a dangerous one in the international debt structure. It is difficult to say which elements were the most important, but it is not a challenge to recognize what happened to the debt markets.

TABLE 7

LDC INDEBTEDNESS TO U.S. AND BRITISH COMMERCIAL BANKS AS A PERCENTAGE OF TOTAL EXTERNAL DEBT, 1981

	Percent of Total Due to U.S. Banks	Percent of Total Due to British Banks	Percent of Total Due to Both
Argentina	33.9	14.1	48.0
Brazil	34.5	12.3	46.9
Mexico	37.6	13.7	51.3
Venezuela	38.5	11.8	50.4
Philippines	50.0	11.8	61.8
Chile	54.3	14.3	68.6
South Korea	45.2	12.6	57.8
Poland	7.8	5.9	13.7
Indonesia	29.2	6.9	36.1
Yugoslavia	24.3	14.0	38.3
Nigeria	18.3	20.0	33.3

Source: Andrew F. Brimmer, The World Banking System: Outlook in a Context of Crisis (New York and London: NYU Press, 1985), Table 3. Cited in Darity and Horn, 1988:187.

One place to start, according to Makin (1984:127-128), is with U.S. policy, particularly with the Carter Administration's policies of 1977 and 1978. The Administration's fiscal policies were designed to stimulate demand in the U.S. economy, but there was relatively little in the way of surplus capital assets that could be readily put to use. The resulting inflation, both in the U.S. and within the global economy, helped LDCs find justification for borrowing additional funds, since they assumed the prices on their commodity exports would continue to rise.

But in 1979, under the leadership of Federal Reserve chair Paul Volcker, the U.S. effectively reversed course and cut demand and the growth of the money supply. This virtually coincided with a second oil price shock in 1979 and 1980 (larger than the first in terms of the amount of funds transferred to OPEC states) (Sjaastad, 1983:309-310). Now there was not the same degree of concern about recycling petrodollars as there had been after the first oil shock. With rising fiscal deficits in developed states, the new OPEC surplus was absorbed by the major economic powers, further cutting the amounts available for the LDCs.

Sjaastad (1983:309-310) isolates three "almost simultaneous" causes behind the debt crunch which occurred in the early 1980s. The first was the rise in the dollar against other currencies in 1980 and early 1981, and its continued strength in 1982. Related to this were two other factors: 1) the dramatic rise in interest rates on dollar deposits, and 2) the sharp fall in the dollar prices for developing states' exports. With most LDC debt denominated in dollars, and pegged to LIBOR in floating rates, the rise in the dollar and dollar interest rates meant an increase in LDC debt service costs. Interest payments rose, and the situation for debtor countries was exacerbated by worsening terms of trade. While real interest rates had been negative through much of the previous decade, by the end of 1980 they had risen into the 15% to 20% range, making it now very possible for developing states "to have too much debt", unlike before.

The second cause Sjaastad finds was the greater tendency of developed states to run large fiscal deficits. This coincided with a rapid decline in OPEC members' current accounts surpluses, starting in early 1981. The superior ability of developed states to borrow to finance their fiscal deficits, combined with a shrinking of the pool of lendable funds, further pressured debtor states which needed money.

The third immediate cause behind the debt crisis was the British-Argentine war over the Falkland Islands in May and June of 1982. American banks that were heavily exposed in Latin America had been operating for some time under the assumption that the U.S. would aid the region if a debt payments emergency took place. The Reagan Administration's decision to side with the British during the war damaged the banks' confidence in that presumption, and precipitated a sharp drop in new lending to the area. To insiders, Mexico's halt in debt service payments in August 1982, and the spread of the crisis to Argentina, Brazil, and Chile by year's end, was not totally unexpected. The other causes were more important, Sjaastad says, but the war exposed the dangers most clearly.

Kuczynski (1983:22-24) also emphasizes the role of miscalculation by both debtors and creditors. From the vantage point of the second oil shock, both misjudged what the world economy would look like in 1981 and 1982. Few observers at the outset of the decade would have predicted the depth of the coming global recession, and its severity in the U.S. Debtor states, Kuczynski writes, were unsuspectingly caught in a "scissors effect", between the declining value of their exports, and the rise in real interest rates for debt service or new loans. Many decision makers assumed that developed states were protected from a severe recession, and that LDCs would recover quickly. Such had been the case after the first oil shock; the recession in the U.S. was comparatively brief, and petrodollars were quickly recycled to

FIGURE 2

**INDICATORS OF DEBT BURDEN
(NON-OIL DEVELOPING COUNTRIES)**

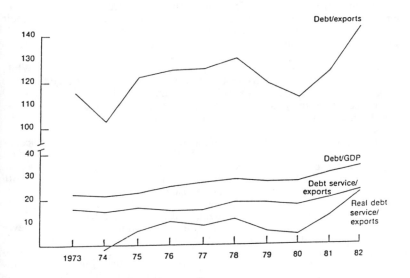

Source: Cline, 1984:5.

developing countries. But in the early 1980s, after the second oil shock, recycling continued, but at a lower rate for the LDCs; the debt was already so high in many states that interest payments alone on debt absorbed 40% to 50% of their export earnings.

These explanations attribute a great deal of responsibility for the debt situation to political decisions and factors. This is not to say that interpretations of a more purely economic nature cannot be found.[3] But the result is the same in any case. According to OECD data, in the boom decade for LDC borrowing, from 1971 to 1982 the total external debt for developing nation-states (including OPEC states) grew 600%, and their debt service burden ballooned by 1100%. This translates to external debt growth of 19% per year in nominal, and 12% per year in real terms (Sjaastad, 1983:306).

The Conditions of Complex Interdependence in
International Debt

In some ways the characteristics of Keohane and Nye's framework are reflected better in international debt than in the issue areas they review. In regard to the declining utility of force, they point out that small states have attempted to use military force to extend their territorial jurisdiction over coastal waters, but that is the only substantial application of force they note in the most recent oceans regime. In monetary affairs Keohane and Nye find no instance of a nation-state applying or threatening force to pursue its goals. While there have been attempts to link progress on monetary arrangements to mutual security objectives (especially between the U.S. and its NATO allies), they find no evidence that monetary powers have seen force as an appropriate resource to use in financial dealings.

In international debt, even the two "uses" of force seen in oceans and money cannot be found. Although the period under study is more brief, no actor can be found attempting to apply military means to gain resources or opportunities in debt negotiations. This includes both creditor and debtor states, and all nonstate actors. Force seems to be especially poorly suited for the pursuit of financial concessions. Even over the question of Poland's debt, with its relevance to the U.S.-U.S.S.R. security struggle, considerations of military security never apparently entered the picture; this was the case both with U.S. dealings with the Polish government, and with Washington's relations with its Japanese and western European allies. This situation certainly was the case with relations between creditor and debtor states; the latter were generally not involved in security arrangements with the former. In short, it seems debtors and creditors were interdependent to a sufficient degree to preclude either attempting to use force to pursue its goals.

These general conclusions about the features of complex interdependence are borne out in the hierarchy of issues found in international debt. In the oceans regime, security was a high priority during the Cold War, but declined over time in favor of economic and ecological concerns. In monetary affairs, money was "high politics" unless some military or security threat existed (a situation which Keohane and Nye intimate is becoming less likely); this means that quite often money was at the top of the international policy agenda.

In international debt, for the bulk of the period under study, debt management was security. For debtor states, MDBs, and private banks, managing the debt "overhang" was as important as any other issue; for some actors such as Mexico and Brazil, it was the foreign policy issue at times. For most debtor countries, military and territorial security was not the concern financial stability was. And for creditor states, including even such skeptics as the U.S. under the Reagan Administration, debt clearly became a very important consideration when dealing with LDCs; many of these countries had no real role to play in the security calculations of major powers.

In terms of the variety of channels of contact among actors, in the oceans regime Keohane and Nye note a rapid increase in the number of IGOs operating, and in their effectiveness in rule-making for the regime. In monetary affairs they argue that the number of IGOs operating has not grown nearly as much as in the oceans regime; a variety of such organizations has been effective for a long period of time, making rules and providing forums for official communication. And in both regimes Keohane and Nye find an increase in nongovernmental contact, as more nonstate actors have involved themselves in policy questions.

The variety of contacts among actors in international debt is probably as broad as can be found in any policy area involving both developed states and LDCs. Lessons from both of Keohane and Nye's test areas can be applied to debt management. For example, international debt has seen little increase in the number of types of nongovernmental actors involved in global economics; international banks have long been active, but now there are more of them. Not only has their number increased, but their importance in creating regime rules has grown, with the development of the "London Club" arrangements for rescheduling sovereign debt owed to private banks (Hudes, 1985). Nor has there been much of an increase in the number of intergovernmental forums, but their roles in making regime rules and facilitating communication among actors have burgeoned greatly. Such forums include the BIS and the IMF, both of whom were instrumental in preventing an international financial collapse in late 1982. The Paris Club, designed as a forum for rescheduling official debts, became more integral to debt management in 1982 (Kettell and Magnus, 1986:148-150). The IMF has continued to be a key actor in debt negotiations since 1982, and the World Bank has become the focus of greater international debate about its role in assisting debtor countries. Interstate contacts that have not taken place under the auspices of particular agencies have increased as well; consider the intermittent LDC discussions about forming a debtor cartel.

The result of these changes has been to make realist assumptions virtually ineffective in providing a framework for understanding how rules are made in the debt management regime. The rise of nongovernmental and intergovernmental actors, and the increase in the number of bureaucracies and departments within individual state governments which can pursue varied objectives, has made regime politics increasingly complex and difficult to study. Overall, contacts that used to be bilateral in nature and importance have become multilateral; the quintessential example is the way in which the Paris and London "Clubs" coordinate efforts to reschedule LDC debt payments (see Lipson, 1981; Hudes, 1985).

The Political Process in International Debt

Keohane and Nye argue three propositions about actor goals in situations of complex interdependence. First, they observe that the goals of states will vary by issue area; this is confirmed in part by the fact that security matters occasionally take second place to other concerns. They also posit that the goals of transnational actors can be expected to differ by issue area, and indicate the evidence clearly supports this. The most important point they claim to make about actors' objectives is that "transnational politics" (1977:115) increase the difficulty states have in pursuing coherent policies. Keohane and Nye suggest that the more harmonized domestic desires are, and the more focused and unified policy elites are on goals, the more coherent and rational state polices can be expected to be. The reverse of this situation is also true: the more fragmented public interests are, the less effort policy makers devote toward seeking their aims, and the less agreement on goals and tactics such people manifest, the smaller will be the chances of coherent policies being designed.

In the debt management regime the first half of this third proposition has been supported. Most governments' (although there is no reason to believe international organizations could not manifest internal differences) inner differences on policy goals and means were relatively minor. As was the case with U.S. policy, the overriding objective for almost all actors was the preservation of the lending system. Even for LDCs which did not particularly like the system, over the short term there was no choice but to maintain it. Hence the disagreements among most actors in the international debt issue area were comparatively minor.

As matters have progressed, the second half of Keohane and Nye's third proposition has not been tested in debt. It is possible that if the debt "crisis" declines in salience on the international and certain domestic policy agendas, fragmented interests will become active, and the metapolicy in support of the regime will lose its consensus. The judgement here is cautiously in support of Keohane and Nye's conclusions on actors' goals.

Keohane and Nye also suggest that in complex interdependence the ability to manipulate interdependence, international organizations, and transnational actors will be the more usual form of power than the capacity to apply force. This is reflected in the politics of the oceans regime, they say. Their conclusions have also proven valid in international debt. Debtor states that have been able to emphasize the interdependence of themselves, other debtors, creditor countries, banks, and MDBs have been the most effective at gaining rescheduling of payments and other concessions; they have used their influence in international organizations to publicize their desires for a changed policy agenda.

The assumptions behind complex interdependence imply that the policy agenda is set in an issue area primarily by the distribution of power in that area, not by the overall systemic distribution. Also important in agenda formation is the capacity of regimes to adjust to economic and technological changes, and shifts in the actors involved. Both the oceans and money regimes have had their agendas centered on responding to broad changes that have pressured the utility of established regime rules, Keohane and Nye indicate. Such has also been the way the agenda has been formed in the relatively young debt management regime. Most regime politics have centered on the need to establish and maintain the structure of the lending and payments system, in conditions in which few actors find it completely to their liking, but are unable to construct a better one.

On the subject of issue linkage, Keohane and Nye believe that combining progress on different issues will be more difficult for actors operating under conditions of complex interdependence than under those of realism. This is because power is no longer effectively seen as a fungible commodity in complex interdependence; power in one issue area does not easily equate to power in another area. Strong states that at one time could link issues will have trouble doing so now, Keohane and Nye suggest. As they expect, small states have had more success linking issues in the oceans regime, because of their voting strength in international organizations. In monetary affairs, strong states have maintained their greater success because of their financial strength; the medium of power is different between the two issue areas.

In international debt, the record indicates that if issue linkage has taken place it has been within the debt management regime. The voting majority LDCs possess in international organizations has been countered by the weighted voting power held by financially prosperous states in other organizations such as the IMF. In fact, most substantive rule making in the debt regime takes place in these single issue organizations in which linking of debt issues to other topics is not likely. In the end, little has changed in debt negotiations. Stronger and richer states cannot dictate regime rules with any assurance of success; nor can they demand excessively rigorous changes in the internal policies of debtors without inviting debt moratoriums or defaults. Neither are debtors able to engineer dramatic changes in the processes or structure of the debt regime.

Hence Keohane and Nye's thoughts on the difficulty of linking issues are confirmed reasonably well. Power remains a function of actor capabilities in specific issue areas; in debt neither creditors nor debtors have resources or assets they have been willing to use to bargain in related areas.

In complex interdependence the role of international organizations will be substantial, Keohane and Nye suggest. In the history of the oceans regime they point to a rise in the number of these actors, and in their importance for rule making. In monetary affairs they report that the situation has largely been static, with little increase seen in the number of international organizations, and little appreciable increase in the influence of LDCs in them. Nonetheless, in both cases international organizations have been influential in a number of ways.

In international debt (as indicated above) there has been no great rush to create multilateral organizations; all the major actors in this category have existed for some time. Creditor states continue to dominate the most important of the rule making organizations, therefore they do not object to addressing debt regime rules in these bodies. But the effectiveness of these actors at rulemaking is mitigated by their lack of enforcement power. The result is that new regime rules are made and old ones are modified largely at the same loci, and by the same actors as before, but _some_ change has taken place. In short, the development of international organizations as major actors in debt has not been as restricted as in monetary affairs, but it has not been as remarkable as in oceans politics.

In summation, it is clear that the distribution of power and the political processes involved in international debt are conceptualized fairly well by the complex interdependence framework. It is also true, though perhaps less obvious, that the "characteristics" of complex interdependence--that is, the structure of capabilities--are more exactly in conformity with the reality of debt politics than is the case with the processes (although the difference is not severe enough to invalidate the application of the general framework). This situation is probably best explained by the fact that the structure of power is a more static concept, one assessed fairly well at a single juncture; the processes of debt management are dynamic in nature and require a longer look than is currently possible in this issue area. Fortunately (or unfortunately, depending upon one's viewpoint) there will probably be ample opportunity for assessing the application of complex interdependence to debt in the future.

A Note on Models of Regime Change

The final portion of Chapter Three reviewed the four models of regime change which Keohane and Nye use to explain shifts in the oceans and money issue areas. The four were the economic process, the overall structure, the issue structure, and the international organization models. Keohane and Nye argue that the history of regime change in their two issue areas indicates that no individual model has always been accurate in explaining shifts in regime dynamics. In fact, when conditions of realism apply, the first two models will be more correct; when conditions of complex interdependence exist the second two will apply more readily (see Table Eight).

Hence, in reviewing the information they have gathered on the oceans and money regimes, Keohane and Nye conclude (1977:161):

1. With respect to trends in the conditions of world politics over the past half century, the complex interdependence ideal type seems to be becoming increasingly relevant. The three most recent cases are all closer to complex interdependence than to realism.

2. With respect to the relevance of theories of world politics, it seems quite clear that traditional theories based on overall structure models and economic process models explain regime change under realist conditions much better than under complex interdependence conditions. The traditional models are particularly weak for explanations of recent cases in which the conditions of complex interdependence, on the whole, applied.

3. These two propositions together imply that traditional theories of world politics, as applied to oceans and monetary politics, are becoming less useful, and that new theories based on issue structure and international organization models will frequently be needed for understanding reality and framing appropriate policies.

These conclusions are based on the history of oceans and monetary regime politics over a half-century period. It is accordingly

TABLE 8

EXPLANATORY POWER OF OVERALL STRUCTURE AND ECONOMIC PROCESS MODELS OF REGIME CHANGE

	Conditions in the Issue Area	
Explanatory Power	Nearer to to Realism	Nearer to Complex Interdependence
High	Oceans, pre-1920 Oceans, 1945-46 Money, 1944-48 Money, 1958	
Low		Money, 1925 Money, 1931 Oceans, 1967 Money, 1971 Money, 1976

Source: Keohane and Nye, 1977:161.

impossible to apply these four models of regime change to international debt, because in debt there has only been one regime change: its creation. Other shifts within debt management have not been sufficiently severe to qualify as changes of regime. But the discussion of the characteristics and the processes of complex interdependence in debt given above provides some room to draw conclusions about the correctness of applying this framework to international debt. The fundamental question at issue here is "Did the forces behind the creation of the debt management regime, and those currently involved in its functioning, reflect conditions of complex interdependence or realism?"

It can be argued that realist models are marginally applicable at best. As for the economic process model, there never occurred a basic shift in the prevailing global economic paradigm. The debt scares of 1982 did not correspond to substantial shifts in the operating rules of the international political economy; no evidence suggests rule changes in world capitalism equivalent to the slow downfall of the free seas regime or the Bretton Woods monetary regime. Mexico's suspension of debt payments may have caused the heart of international banking to skip a beat, but there was no heart transplant. And as for the overall structure model, which expects military and political hegemons to have a dominant role in most issue areas, no state--including the U.S.--could do much more than lead rule making in debt management; domination was clearly impossible.

The complex interdependence models fare somewhat better in explaining regime creation and function. The issue structure model assumes power will most likely accrue to the actor with resources unique to a particular issue area. As was the case in oceans politics, in which some LDCs and transnational actors had exceptional resources for use, in debt certain debtor countries (such as Mexico and Brazil) possessed sufficient power to frustrate creditors and MDBs intent on mandating particular austerity policies in these states. The perverse situation arose in which the more heavily indebted nation-states gained a large voice in negotiations with creditors. On the other side of the issue, commercial banks and MDBs also had unique resources, including their knowledge and position within the issue area; this gave them specific capabilities to mediate between creditor and debtor states.

The international organization model partially supports the complex interdependence model also. Debtor countries had perhaps their greatest voice in the UN General Assembly, UNCTAD, and informal forums such as the Cancun Conference; their difficulty was an inability to gain a dominant position in organizations where creditor states and banks had the power to set the agenda. Nonetheless, the ability of LDCs to set the agenda in certain forums was useful, especially in building communications networks among debtors (see Chapter Nine on the move for a "debtor cartel").

Far too little can be said as yet about the applicability of models of regime change to international debt. But the evidence available further supports the claim that realism cannot sufficiently explain regime dynamics in this issue area.

Modeling Complex Interdependence in Foreign Policy

To this point, complex interdependence has been applied as a framework to interpret politics in the oceans, money, and debt issue areas. On balance, Keohane and Nye's framework functions to capture the structure of power and political processes in debt management approximately as well as it does in the other issue areas.

The discussion has shown how Keohane and Nye have attempted to answer the first major question of their text: What are the major features of world politics when interdependence, particularly economic interdependence, is extensive? It has also revealed how they deal with their second question: How and why do international regimes change?

Despite the connection with oceans, money, and debt, Keohane and Nye's approach--as they indicate--is developed at the systemic level. Their model does not deal with the possibility of recognizing complex interdependence at the level of specific foreign policies. To argue that conditions of complex interdependence existed at the systemic level, and then to assume such conditions dictated <u>policies</u>, is only a partial test of this alternative to realism. A stronger case is to be made by developing from the foregoing conclusions a profile of the policies and actions expected by states in complex interdependence, then studying foreign policies to see if such efforts do indeed appear. This would constitute a step toward constructing a conceptual model of foreign policy in complex interdependence. Given the emphasis on realism in contemporary international relations theory, most scholars have at least an intuitive understanding of what type of policies states are expected to pursue in realist conditions; complex interdependence has heretofore not had similar attention.

The Structure of Complex Interdependence and Policy

The condition of being interdependent with other actors provides states with new policy making opportunities, and also constrains their options. Much depends on the ability of state officials to recognize their nation-state's situation, especially if it differs significantly from previous assumptions.

<u>The role of force</u>. Obviously, the weaker the state the less likely it will be to use force, if it expects stronger actors to respond in kind. More important, however, is the expectation that the greater the degree of mutual dependence among actors--that is, interdependence--the

less likely will be the chances actors will apply military means in
pursuit of goals. The more issues in which states share such a
relationship, the less likely will they each be to damage general ties
over narrow differences that do not threaten basic values.

This is not to say that some states may not prefer, or even
attempt, to use force. But the more pervasive the mutual dependence,
and the greater the depth of its recognition among policy making elites,
the less likely is force to be a credible threat. Policy makers may
attempt to tie agreements on nonsecurity issues to issues of mutual
defense (as in monetary affairs), but this is actually far removed from
the realist suggestion that military prowess is a commodity readily
applied for settling disagreements.

Absence of a hierarchy of issues. As Keohane and Nye show in
monetary politics, military security may rise to the top of the policy
agenda in times of external threat. In the final analysis, the
territorial integrity of a state is a paramount goal, and one of the
reasons for a state's existence. But in situations of complex
interdependence, as often as not other issues--either as broad as
"economic prosperity" or as narrow as "international debt"--will serve
as high politics. Security in the traditional sense does not disappear
from concern; rather it is held in abeyance. Decision makers in
interdependent states will have in mind their own hierarchies of issues;
the more accurately government officials in one state recognize and
share hierarchies held by leaders in other states, the more likely they
will be able to pursue mutually beneficial policies. The reverse is
also expected, of course.

Multiple channels of contact. In complex interdependence, all
actors will have to face a large variety of other actors. With the
breaking of the dominance of military security, and the concomitant rise
of other issues, new actors will be bound to complicate the policy
agenda in almost any issue area. Policy making will become more complex
than in realist conditions, and may require more effort by decision
makers to design and maintain coherent policies. If actors do not
realize the variety of forces involved, their miscalculation will lead
to their efforts being frustrated. Moreover, the novelty of these
situations may lengthen the time involved in the search for appropriate
policies and the means to pursue them.

The Political Process in Complex Interdependence

The particular distribution of power just mentioned also suggests
unique processes by which resources are translated into policies.

Actor goals. The higher an issue is on the national policy agenda,
the more attention it can be expected to receive from policy elites.
The chances of rational, interrelated policy goals being promulgated

increase with the amount of attention being given by the decision making elites. All other things remaining equal (admittedly a dangerous assumption), if this happens the chances of policy success increase.

Policy instruments. For the reasons mentioned in the previous section, force will rarely be utilized. For interdependent states, the requirements for successful policies have changed. Contemporary state leaders will need to recognize these changes, and devote resources to 1) measuring the amount of interdependence which exists in an issue area, and finding ways to affect that, 2) keeping close tabs on transnational actors, and 3) taking an active role in international organizations, if not to dictate policies at least to lead in their development.

Agenda formation. Under more modern conditions, the political agenda will be set by the distribution of power in particular issue areas, and by the ability of regimes to adjust to the demands placed on them by events and actors. It can be expected that former hegemons will experience difficulty in setting the agenda, as the importance of regimes invites participation by previously marginal actors. This will necessitate a period of adjustment for former systemic leaders; substantial stress is anticipated in their policy making apparatuses until their previous goals and preconceptions are brought into line with modern reality. Mistakes in setting goals and assigning means to achieving those objectives may be common until the objective and subjective situations are brought into rough equivalence.

Linking of issues. Because of the variety of types of power, and the number of actors with influence on the policy agenda, it may be difficult for states to link issues. States usually considered strong will have problems in this area; their greatest successes will come in dealings with other actors with whom it is mutually dependent, and in a number of issue areas. But because force is unusable, and actors can get resources from different places and actors, linkage of issues may more appropriately be considered a bonus, not something which can be intentionally pursued. More successful in economic and political terms will be states whose decision makers recognize these restrictions; if they do not policy failures can be especially costly in lost reputation.

Role of international organization. The role of international organizations has much to do with the variety of types of power in existence. In some organizations such as the UN, voting strength is sufficient for states which share goals to have power. In other organizations such as the IMF and the World Bank, other assets under the control of individual states equate with power. Participation may be high in organizations of both extremes, but states--especially those new to the understanding of complex interdependence--will reserve the right to opt out of the requirements of these organizations. This reflects the fact that complex interdependence does not expect states to surrender any sovereignty to multilateral bodies.

Endnotes

[1] On the development of the Eurodollar market see Charles Lipson, "The International Organization of Third World Debt", International Organization 35 (Autumn 1981); and Karen Hudes, "Coordination of Paris and London Club Reschedulings", New York University Journal of International Law and Politics 17 (Spring 1985).

[2] Another factor Makin cites for the increased ability of U.S. banks to lend to other countries is the break with the gold standard (1984:24).

[3] For a brief discussion of economic explanations of the debt situation see Miles Kahler, "Politics and International Debt: Explaining the Debt Crisis" in Miles Kahler, ed. The Politics of International Debt, Ithaca: Cornell University Press, 1986.

CHAPTER SIX

POLAND: THE FIRST DOMINO?

Most popular and scholarly works on international debt date the beginning of the global debt problem from late 1982, when Mexico nearly defaulted on its external obligations. This is simple to understand. For many people, especially Americans, Mexico's effort to restructure its debt provided them with their first exposure to the magnitude of the global debt situation. Mexico's external debt was large, and many U.S. banks were heavily exposed there. The country's financial situation had gone unnoticed by many observers who could reasonably have been expected to be aware of it. The result was that Mexico's troubles in the late summer and fall of 1982 provide a convenient place for the unsophisticated to mark the start of the "debt crisis".

As shown in Chapter Five, discussions of the recent history of international debt could also start in the 1970s, with the rapid growth in international lending fostered by the OPEC oil price increases. One could also begin by studying the rise in debt reschedulings which took place late in that decade, which indicated LDCs were experiencing difficulties in matching the needs of their development programs with the necessities of paying their bills. Such a discussion could then include the inability of developing states to deal with the added strains imposed by the second oil price shocks of 1979 and 1980.

However one wishes to start an investigation of international debt, it would be a mistake to omit Poland's experiences in the early 1980s in seeking additional loans and rescheduling old ones. By the end of 1980, Poland's total external debt had reached $25 billion (see Table Nine), and its debt owed to foreign private banks was the fourth highest in the world (see Figure Three). By early 1982, Poland was experiencing serious difficulties getting additional funds from western governments and banks, and in the previous three years had more of its external debt rescheduled than any other state (see Table Ten).

In fact, two observations about Poland's debt problems are relevant to an understanding of the international debt issue area, and to attempts to apply a complex interdependence interpretation to it.

First, the magnitude of Poland's foreign debt, and the problems it had juggling its obligations in 1980 and 1981 brought international debt to its most prominent position yet on the international agenda. By 1980, the prospect of a large-scale sovereign default began to disturb the previously tranquil nature of international lending, and served notice to interested observers that debt difficulties were not exclusively the province of Third World states.

Second, the Polish situation helped to reveal that by the end of 1981 money center banks as a group had become--at least in some situations--as important as nation-states in determining the politics of international debt. For example, in early 1981 Poland's major sovereign creditors agreed to reschedule most of that country's official debt. Private banks, however, took months longer to accomplish the same task, despite pressure from their home governments. The result was an additional lesson in the creation of a new class of actor within an issue area, with particular capabilities that prevent other actors from restraining it to any great extent. In fact, the increase in influence which commercial banks experienced during Poland's efforts to reschedule its debt may have been as dramatic as that which they felt during the heady days of petrodollar recycling. Governments were to learn that policy making on debt was increasingly difficult, since commercial banks could have policies very much opposed to those of governments. Indirectly, but in a very real sense, when in 1982 the Reagan Administration was forced to pay off loans to Poland which it had guaranteed, it was in part because it could not encourage private banks to lend more.

This chapter is divided into two portions. The first reviews Poland's efforts in 1981 to reschedule its debt; special emphasis is placed on the growth in power of private banks. The second covers the Reagan Administration's decision not to force Poland into default on its obligations to U.S. banks. This is the first of the four "puzzles" of Administration debt policy outlined in Chapter One.

Warsaw, the West, and the Banks

In the history of post-World War II Europe, Poland has never been an economic powerhouse. In the last two decades, Poland's most prosperous period came in the early 1970s, when it appeared to be an attractive target for outside investment. Between 1970 and 1973 Poland's economy actually performed better than that of the Soviet Union. For example, between 1971 and 1975, net industrial production rose nearly 11% per year. Real industrial wages between 1961 and 1970 rose at an average annual rate of 1.8% per year; in 1971 and 1972 they increased 7.2% per year (Bialer, 1981:525). But there was a downside to Poland's industrialization program, and that was the relative deemphasis on the production of consumer goods. The increase in the average Pole's disposable income, coupled with the generally static level of consumer goods available, resulted in a rapid rise in consumer prices. The Polish government responded with price controls and food price subsidies, in an

TABLE 9

POLAND: ECONOMIC INDICATORS
(Billion dollars and percentages)

	1973	1974	1975	1976	1977	1978	1979	1980	1981	1982
Exports	2.5	3.9	4.1	4.4	4.9	5.5	6.3	7.5	5.4	5.2
Imports	4.0	6.0	7.4	7.5	7.1	7.5	8.8	9.1	6.0	4.0
Current Account	-1.3	-2.2	-3.1	-3.2	-2.4	-2.5	-2.8	-2.6	-3.0	-1.8
Reserves	.6	.5	.6	.8	.4	.9	1.2	.6	.8	1.1
Total Debt	2.8	4.6	8.0	11.5	14.0	17.8	22.7	25.0	26.4	26.6
Short-term debt	1.5	2.2	2.7	2.8	2.6	2.8	4.1	3.1	2.8	2.7
Net debt/exports	88.5	105.6	180.0	242.7	276.2	308.6	341.3	324.9	469.2	491.0
Inflation	2.6	6.7	3.0	4.4	4.9	8.7	6.7	10.0	37.0	92.7

Source: Jan Vanous, Centrally Planned Economies Current Analysis, vol. 3, nos. 31-32, 38-39, 69-70; Richard Portes, The Polish Crisis: Western Policy Options; Zbigniew M. Fallenbuchl, "The Polish Economy at the Beginning of the 1980s": David D. Driscoll, "Sovereign Debt: The Polish Example"; Central Intelligence Agency, Handbook of Economic Statistics, 1982. Cited in Cline, 1984, p. 274.

Note: Exports and imports with non-socialist countries. Current account balance in convertible currencies. Net debt as percentage of merchandise exports to nonsocialist countries.

FIGURE 3

EXTERNAL BANK DEBT OF FIVE MAJOR DEBTOR STATES, 1976-1986 (Owed to BIS-Reporting Banks)

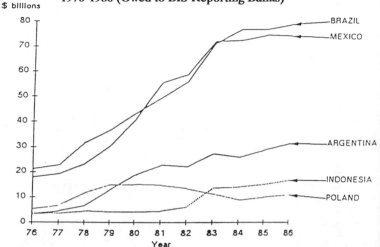

Source: BIS, <u>International Banking and Financial Market Developments</u>. Cited in Bouchet, 1987:30.

attempt in the mid-1970s to keep inflation from becoming uncontrollable and adding to labor unrest.

Poland therefore found itself facing the same economic constraints that afflicted Third World states in the middle to late 1970s. The oil price increases which drove prices up in the developed world, and caused a recession in the west, forced a major reduction by 1975 in Poland's exports, without a corresponding decline in the country's imports and consumer demand (Strausz-Hupe, 1981:64). The loss in export income and the government's simultaneous insistence on pursuing industrial development helped stimulate a four-fold increase in external debt between 1973 and 1975 (Cline, 1984:274). In fact, as early as 1975 some observers were having second thoughts about the advisability of making new loans to Poland; some suggested the nation's economy would need to be substantially reformed if the country was to avoid an eventual collapse. Nonetheless, banks continued to lend; between 1976 and 1980 Poland's external debt doubled. As was the case with lending to LDCs (see Chapter Five), a number of factors worked against any real reduction in new loans. While some banks (especially in the U.S.) reduced their lending to Poland, others from Japan and western Europe, with petrodollar deposits to loan, eagerly took up the slack. Western governments' export agencies continued to guarantee credits to Poland. Many government and private bank officials assumed that a Soviet "umbrella" existed over Council of Mutual Economic Assistance (CMEA) nations, which would prevent them from defaulting on western loans ("Polish", 1982:10).

By 1979 the Polish situation was a significant concern for lenders, who no longer looked for reasons to ignore warning signs.

TABLE 10

DEBT RELIEF EXTENDED TO DEVELOPING COUNTRIES 1979-1982
(First Quarter)

	Percent Rescheduled		Total Rescheduled (million $)
	Commercial Banks	Paris Club	
Poland	49	51	4,900
Turkey	73	27	4,383
Romania	78	22	3,540
Costa Rica	99	1	869
Nicaragua	76	24	762
Zaire	77	23	517
Jamaica	100	0	553
Sudan	89	11	503
Bolivia	100	0	460
Pakistan	0	100	186

Source, The Economist, March 20, 1982, p. 9.

Note: Romania's total includes arrearages from 1981 of $500 million to commercial banks and $40 million to Paris Club lenders. Seven LDCs had $20 million or less rescheduled.

Despite a general lack of hard evidence about the internal functioning of Poland's economy, the data which was available suggested the country's industrialization campaign was failing. Depressed conditions in western nations reduced Poland's exports of copper and coal, without a concomitant reduction in imports ("Polish", 1982:10). Growing labor unrest over industrial wages and the availability of goods prevented the government from raising prices and restricting demand (Strausz-Hupe, 1981:61-62). By the end of the decade signs of impending collapse could be found. The GNP growth rate, which had been 3.0% in 1978, had plummeted to -2.3% in 1979. Poland's net hard currency indebtedness rose from $14.3 billion in 1977, to $16.9 billion in 1978, and to $20.5 billion by the end of 1979 (Fallenbuchl, 1982:7). In both 1979 and 1980 Poland's national income (measured in absolute terms) fell; it was the only Soviet bloc state to experience such a decline. In August and September of 1980, Polish officials reported, industrial production was 17% lower than for the same period in 1979. In the first three quarters of 1980, only 37% of the country's construction plan for the year was fulfilled, and similarly disappointing figures were found for grain and meat production (Bialer, 1981:524).

Only for a short time could some banks brush aside their concerns over Poland's credit standing. In March 1979 Bank of America led the creation of a syndicated loan of $550 million; this was actually oversubscribed from the target amount of $500 million. But by now Poland was quietly approaching western governments with requests for new loans and credits. Stopgap measures by France and West Germany provided some assistance, but by April 1980 representatives of Bank Handlowy, Poland's foreign trade bank, had to approach private banks for another set of funds. For most observers, it was obvious that Poland' overtures to Bank of America and West Germany's Dresdner Bank were really applications for rescue packages. Poland's economy continued to deteriorate further, and bankers were unwilling to believe its government's economic forecasts. Poland's 1979 current account deficit was twice what had been predicted, and Warsaw's projection for 1980 met with skepticism.

Bank of America and Dresdner Bank had difficulty arranging new financing. Bank of America's original target was $500 million, but it could only draw together $375 million. Even this required an $80 million contribution from Moscow Narodny Bank and the Polish bank Pekao. The $500 million package arranged by Dresdner required substantial pressure from the German finance ministry on German banks, and a government guarantee on 40% of it ("Polish", 1982:10,15; see also Tagliabue, 1980).

In November 1980 Poland requested an additional $8 to 12 billion in new loans from western governments, including $3 billion in low interest loans from the U.S. (Gwertzman, 1980; also Oberdorfer, 1980). But the reluctance now pervading private bank officials was being felt in western governments; the outgoing Carter Administration responded with an offer for only $670 million in loan guarantees (Seligman, 1980:112). It was clear by the end of 1980 that Poland had few willing benefactors in western financial circles.

In a very real sense, then, 1981 appeared to loom as a crucial year for Poland. Events had suggested, and would in the future, that Poland, western governments, and commercial banks were now locked in an interdependent relationship. Poland's efforts in 1981 to reschedule its official and private debts revealed 1) the ability of a small state to influence the condition of the global economy (even if that state was not an integral part of that economy), and 2) the relative power of the banks--and small clusters of banks within the larger group--to obstruct government policies. The efforts of both governments and private banks to reschedule Poland's debts illustrate the dramatic changes taking place in the politics of international debt.

Very little needs to be said about Poland's efforts in early 1981 to reschedule its debt owed to western state governments, because the process was very simple and straightforward. The G-15[1] governments, which held the largest shares of Polish official debt, met under the auspices of the Paris Club during the spring of 1981. In late April they reached an agreement to allow Poland to postpone $2.6 billion in debt payments due in 1981. In exchange for agreeing to implement austerity measures, Poland had its 1981 debt payments delayed until 1986, after which they would be spread over four years. These funds only amounted to approximately one-fourth of the debt relief Poland needed for the year, but the G-15 representatives expected western banks to provide further relief by rescheduling $3 billion in 1981 bank debt payments (Lewis, 1981a).

West Germany and the U.S. were heavily involved in efforts at this point to avoid a Polish default. Early in January West Germany had guaranteed $153 million in new bank loans to Poland (Tagliabue, 1981a); as the state with the largest share of public and private funds at risk in Poland the Bonn government believed it had little choice ("West's Stake", 1981:49). The U.S., foreshadowing the action it would adopt a year later, in February 1981 allowed Poland to delay repayment on more than $80 million of Commodity Credit Corporation (CCC) credits due between March 1 and June 30 (Oberdorfer, 1981:A1,A6; "U.S. Lets Poland",1981). By the beginning of May 90% of Poland's official debt for 1981 had been rescheduled. Clearly western governments did not wish to push Warsaw to the brink of default.

In contrast to the process involved in avoiding a Polish default on its official obligations, the operation to reschedule Warsaw's debts to private banks in 1981 was lengthy, difficult, and demonstrated that a number of banks were not immediately willing to follow the G-15's lead. The Economist reported the story of the banks' 'brinkmanship' ("The Polish Bogey", 1982:10, 15-16, 21-22); what follows in large measure summarizes that report.

As 1981 began Polish officials apparently did not anticipate severe problems in continuing to borrow from foreign banks. Despite suggestions from western bankers that Poland begin to restructure its debts, and with banks refusing to rollover short-term credits to Poland, Bank Handlowy representatives spent most of January and February asking U.S. and European bankers for a new $1 billion loan. Unaware of the extent of the change in mood among western financial experts, Poland's officials even called representatives of seventy banks to a meeting in London, at which they renewed their request for the $1 billion loan, and asked for rescheduling. But Poland could find no takers, and the initiative passed to the banks.

A twenty-bank task force of Poland's largest private creditors was set up to represent 501 banks to which Poland owed funds. At the end of March the Poles were informed that they would have to negotiate with the task force. Poland by now was in technical default on its loans. The only factor preventing widespread financial catastrophe was that no large creditor was willing to call in Warsaw's loans, which would have triggered cross-default provisions on other funds. Little in the way of Polish assets was available for western banks to seize; the banks had little choice but to continue talks ("Polish", 1982:16).

Aggravating the situation was a severe split among banks. Polish representatives asked for a delay on principal payments due between March 27 and June 30 while negotiations proceeded. Bankers divided into hard-line and soft-line groups (Portes, 1981). In the first camp were those (such as the Swiss) who demanded prompt payment of all short-term debts, and some (especially Americans) who suggested charging penalty interest rates on overdue debt. In the second group were a number of banks, especially West German ones, whose exposure was relatively great; they favored a more conciliatory approach.

Because of their strategic position as the holders of the largest portion of Poland's commercial bank debt (Tagliabue, 1981b), the West Germans were able to pressure representatives from other countries. At meetings in London in mid-April, the soft-line position triumphed. Second quarter debts were delayed. The bankers created a five-bank working group to outline rescheduling terms, and a committee of international economists to assess the state of the Polish economy.

Early in May the working group and Polish negotiators met in New York ("Polish, 1982:15-16). The Poles insisted that the banks follow the lead of the recently concluded Paris Club discussions and reschedule all principal and interest due the banks in 1981. The bankers immediately refused. Rescheduling principal was possible, they said, but the interest would have to be paid on time. In retrospect, the Poles should have anticipated this. Banks which are not receiving interest payments on loans are often required to place these obligations in a "non-performing funds" category; this means they must be written down against profits. Any chance of an early agreement on Poland's private debts was unlikely.

Late in May the obstacle toward progress again turned out to be the banks. At Dresdner Bank's offices in Frankfurt the working group revealed its proposal to the full task force. It involved rescheduling 95% of the $2.4 billion due banks in the last three quarters of 1981 over seven and one-half years, starting in 1986. Interest on the rescheduled portion would be 1.75% over LIBOR, which was hovering around 16.75%. A penalty of 2.75% would be assessed on late payments, and a 1% renegotiation fee would be charged. But again banks were split. One the one side were those, usually Americans, who demanded more information about Poland's economy and its recovery program. On the other were those, usually Europeans, who favored approval of the working group's already stringent proposal. Bankers in Frankfurt could not resolve the issue, and decided to let their national task forces take the matter to the 501 individual banks.

At this point representatives of some American banks almost brought the entire rescheduling effort to a halt. Largely ignoring the Reagan Administration's encouragement that they join their European colleagues in giving Poland some room to maneuver (Bourne, 1981), American bankers decided after the Frankfurt talks that European banks had been far too easy on Poland, and were being unrealistic in accepting Warsaw's predictions of an improvement in its debt service capacity. In voting by bankers, Bank of America was replaced as the leader of the U.S. task force by Bankers Trust, which was given a mandate to push for tougher conditions on Poland (Martin, 1981).

The multinational task force reconvened in Paris at the end of June. U.S. demands for stricter monitoring of the Polish economy and on punitive measures if Poland did not agree to rapid restructuring met European insistence that an agreement had to be reached quickly if default was to be avoided. The result was a series of informal discussions over the next month designed to close the gap between the two extremes. Finally, in Zurich on July 22 bankers reached an agreement (Fouquet, 1981). Warsaw would have to create a committee to work with the banks' "economic steering committee", and would be expected to make quarterly reports once an agreement was finalized. American demands that Poland divulge the source of its Soviet-bloc loans were dealt with by asking Warsaw to release the total amounts of its CMEA funds, but not from where they came. And the banks did agree that Poland would have to be current on its interest payments by December 10, the deadline for signing the entire agreement ("Polish", 1982:16).

The issue now was getting Poland to agree to the proposal. Little was accomplished in meetings between the task force and Poland's representatives during August and September, with the Poles attempting to divide banks into the hard- and soft-line camps. Negotiators even considered agreeing to Warsaw's request for easier terms on rescheduled amounts, but the individual banks would not acquiesce ("Polish", 1982:16). By the middle of September it appeared that there might be no common ground that would prevent a Polish default, and western banks were openly concerned about the possibility of a domino effect among debtor countries, both in eastern Europe and in the Third World. The closest thing to a real crisis in Poland's debt problems came in late September. A task force meeting originally set for September 17 in Vienna was postponed until September 28 because the Poles were not ready. When the meeting finally took place, Polish negotiators had virtually none of the economic data bankers had been expecting since the tentative agreement was reached in July. After a day spent haggling in Vienna, some American members of the task force suggested a meeting in Warsaw with the Polish finance minister. The Polish negotiators objected, saying the minister was occupied "with affairs of state" and that no commercial flights were scheduled to Warsaw the following day. According to The Economist, "The Americans replied that they had 'a private plane waiting at Vienna airport, and that [the finance minister] had better cancel his appointments or there might not be a state left to run'" ("Polish", 1982:21).

The next day, September 29, seven task force members flew to Warsaw and met with the finance minister, Marian Krzak. According to insiders, the bankers told Krzak that Poland would be declared in default on its loans if it did not agree to the task force's conditions. In Vienna the next day the Polish negotiators agreed to the arrangement banks had designed in July.

As events would have it, Poland and its creditors were still not done dealing with Warsaw's 1981 debts. Poland was required to pay $500 million in interest charges on its 1981 debt before the end of the year for the rescheduling arrangement to be finalized (Bennett, 1981c:A1). In mid-December Poland requested a $350 million loan from western banks to be used toward the interest payment (Rowe, 1981:D14). The banks flatly refused (Lewis, 1981c; Tagliabue, 1981d); many of them believed that with Poland's martial law crackdown on the Solidarity labor movement the Soviet Union would be forced to aid Poland, especially with the amount in question so small. By the first week of 1982, Poland indeed did produce $350 million toward the total, supporting the banks' suspicion that a Soviet umbrella did extend to its CMEA allies. In any case, it was not until the middle of April 1982 that Poland was able to clear its entire 1981 interest commitment to western banks, and the banks allowed Poland to stand in undeclared default the entire time.

Realism, Reality, and the Polish Debt

In retrospect, the role of the Reagan Administration in the 'Polish debt crisis' was limited, and it is not surprising that it never gained much attention. But the actions taken by the Reagan Administration in early 1982 help reveal the reduction in governments' autonomy and policy flexibility that accompanied the rescheduling of Poland's debt in 1981. In this broader context, this first "puzzle" of Administration debt policy is easier to understand.

Throughout its first year in office the Reagan Administration kept a close watch on the events in Poland, with the growth of labor unrest and the Solidarity labor movement. By late in the year the Administration was indicating to the Soviet Union that it held the Soviets ultimately responsible for whatever took place in Poland, and that the U.S. could be expected to respond if repressive measures were taken against Poland (see Ash, 1984).

On December 13 the Jaruzelski government in Warsaw imposed martial law, and the Reagan Administration responded with sanctions against Poland and the Soviet Union. At a meeting in Brussels in early January, the U.S. prodded NATO foreign ministers to agree to halt discussions on rescheduling Poland's 1982 debt to western governments (Cody, 1982; Tagliabue, 1982b:D19). The U.S. also ended subsidized food shipments to Poland, and halted U.S. guarantees of new bank credits to Warsaw; it also stopped Polish fishing rights in U.S. territorial waters (Cohen, 1985:136).[2] But reaction in the U.S. as to the severity of these measures was mixed, and many critics of the Administration said the actions were not enough to punish the Jaruzelski regime or the Soviet Union.

Not surprisingly, Reagan officials continued to look for ways to respond to martial law. Economic means seemed to be the main avenue, especially with the Polish economy in a shambles. Poland's economy in late 1981 was in dire need of Soviet assistance. The value (in constant prices) of the country's industrial production in November was 9.4% below the figure for the previous November, and the statistic for December declined further to 25.4% under the total for the same month a year earlier (Fallenbuchl, 1982:17). Warsaw's attempts at genuine economic reform were faltering, and the Reagan Administration believed the Soviet Union could not allow a complete Polish collapse. This version of the umbrella theory assumed that actions which punished the Polish government would indirectly sanction Moscow as well.

One option seized upon by some in the Administration had to do with U.S. bank credits which Warsaw was late in repaying. Over the previous three years the Commodity Credit Corporation (CCC), a branch of the Agriculture Department, had been guaranteeing private bank credits to Poland that Warsaw could use to purchase American farm commodities (Cowan, 1982a:A1; Morgan, 1982b:A11). By early January 1982 Poland owed $3 billion to U.S. banks in this arrangement, with $1.6 billion of the total guaranteed by the CCC (Cohen, 1985:137). Since Poland had not been making its payments, it was in technical default on the entire amount.

Given the Administration's past rhetoric, it perhaps would not have surprised very many observers if Reagan officials had allowed the U.S. banks to declare a Polish default, which was legally required before CCC-guaranteed funds could be repaid by the federal government. President Reagan, Secretary of State Haig, Secretary of Defense

Weinberger, U.N. Ambassador Jeane Kirkpatrick, and CIA Director William Casey all supported sanctions on the issue of Polish martial law (Smith, 1982a:A1; 1982b). But the near collapse of the debt management system the previous year had signalled to the Administration the variety of actors--both sovereign states and commercial banks--which could be hurt if Poland defaulted on its debts. Reagan officials therefore proceeded cautiously.

Discussions within the Administration over U.S. options started early in January, and involved interagency meetings among sub-cabinet level officials (Lipsky, 1982; Cowan, 1982a:D3). The participants included Beryl Sprinkel, Undersecretary of the Treasury for Monetary Affairs; Lionel H. Olmer, Undersecretary of Commerce for International Trade; Robert D. Hormats, Assistant Secretary of State for Economic and Business Affairs; Fred C. Iklè, Undersecretary of Defense for Policy; Richard E. Lyng, Deputy Secretary of Agriculture; and Norman Bailey of the National Security Council (Gelb, 1982:A9).

On one side were arguments in favor of requiring the banks to declare a Polish default before receiving federal assistance. Operating under the assumptions that a Soviet umbrella existed over Poland, those in favor of this position suggested Moscow could simply not afford to let Poland default, because the result would be a cutoff of further western funds to Warsaw and probably to other CMEA states as well. In addition, forcing a default declaration would indirectly punish Moscow for the martial law decision in Poland. Only Iklè and Weinberger were solidly behind this approach (Gelb, 1982:A9; Smith, 1982b).

On the other side of the debate was a softer line, one which explored possibilities of avoiding a default call by banks. A number of officials were not sure a Soviet umbrella really existed, since it appeared that recent Soviet credits to Poland were being used for the purchase of Soviet goods, not for the repayment of debts (Farnsworth, 1982a:D3). Administration decision makers were unwilling to risk the additional hardships for the Polish public which were expected if western aid stopped. The U.S.' European allies opposed a default call, especially since they were far more financially exposed in Poland than the U.S. (see Table Eleven). West Germany put especially severe pressure on the Reagan Administration for a conciliatory approach, since a default could cost the Bonn government $2 billion in guarantees it had made to West German banks (Cowan, 1982:D3).

Some Administration officials openly worried about a default "contagion" (Cohen, 1985:138) if Poland came up short on its debts. In early January both Romania and Yugoslavia experienced difficulties in obtaining short-term funds (Morgan, 1982a; see also Soloman, 1982). In mid-January two U.S. banks, Marine Midland Bank of New York and Fidelity Bank of Philadelphia, placed its Polish loans in the "nonperforming assets" category, although they did not write down the loans as losses (Bennett, 1982a:D1). As of mid-January, no bank had declared a Polish

TABLE 11

HOLDERS OF POLAND'S DEBT
(Million $)

	Total	Commercial Banks
Germany	4,056	1,919
United States	3,053	1,158
France	2,592	882
Austria	1,817	308
Britain	1,781	631
Italy	1,088	338
Japan	1,063	706
Canada	989	323
Switzerland	623	361
Netherlands	304	241
Other Western Countries	3,785	2,033
CMEA Countries	2,271	2,197
Total	23,422	11,097

Source: Business Week, December 28, 1981, p. 49.

default, but Reagan officials knew that if a single large bank did, cross-default clauses could conceivably stimulate other banks to do so.

In the end, a solid majority of Administration officials decided that some other option besides default would have to be found. Both State and Treasury Department officials argued there would be no practical benefit to the U.S. in a Polish default; if American banks declared a default the Poles could simply pay European banks enough to forestall a similar decision there. A default would also close off any possibility Poland would keep making interest or principal payments, no matter how small in size. A default would virtually doom Poland's application to join the IMF, which had been pending for months; such a move was considered ideal by some Administration officials because it would allow a closer look at Poland's internal economy (Cowan, 1982:A1,D3). What may have turned the argument was a confidential cable sent to the State Department by former Federal Reserve Board chair Arthur Burns, then serving as U.S. Ambassador to West Germany. Burns reportedly suggested that the ramifications of a Polish default would be felt with or without a formal declaration to that effect, and that such results would be easier to deal with if they were spread over a number of years; in the interim banks could gain funds to cover their losses. A reduction in western lending to the Soviet bloc had already started, Burns said; if the reduction was too severe it could result in a wave of defaults that would severely pressure the banks and by implication western governments ("Burns Cable", 1982).

In early February the Reagan Administration paid $71 million dollars in guarantees to U.S. banks that had extended Poland credits through the CCC, and put in place a policy that could require the payment of $396.6 million for that purpose in 1982 alone (Cowan, 1982:A1). For all practical purposes, the Administration rewrote U.S. law, by absolving banks of the requirement to declare a default before applying for federal relief. More importantly, as one observer described it, the Reagan Administration "unilaterally rescheduled a portion of Poland's debt", and it did so largely without conditions (Cohen, 1985:138).

The decision did not go unquestioned in Washington. Efforts were made in both the Senate and the House to force a resumption of the previous policy, although both attempts failed (Morgan and Hornblower, 1982). In the following months a variety of Administration officials spoke at various forums in support of the idea that the Administration was taking the hard-line with Poland and the Soviet Union, and that not letting Poland default was a way to 'keep Poland's feet to the fire' (see Gelb, 1982:A1; Seib, 1982; Macnamar, 1982).

By mid-June the Administration had paid, as quietly as possible, $177 million to U.S. banks for CCC-guaranteed loans to Poland (King, 1982b). And by March of the following year the federal government had paid $466 million to avoid a Polish default (Hosendolph, 1983). By then, of course, the amounts at risk in Latin America made such amounts seen small indeed.

Conclusions

The Polish debt problems reveal some important points in the effort to understand how international debt was managed in the first half of the 1980s. Poland's plight was an early indication of the danger to global financial stability which even a relatively small amount of external debt could pose, and the risk of default which could develop when even a comparatively small share of a state's debt needed to be rescheduled. The Polish case also showed the difficulty of avoiding disaster, when a variety of actors with diverging agendas were unable to agree on the severity of the problem at hand. In retrospect, some of the lessons which could have been learned from the Polish case about the tactics needed to mount rescue operations for sovereign debtors were forgotten (see Kempe, 1982); by the time Mexico's condition reached the crisis point in late 1982 most of the history of Poland's debt scare was dismissed as irrelevant.

The efforts to avoid a Polish debt default also highlight the rise of 'new actors' and 'new issues' which bolster a complex interdependence interpretation of systemic politics and foreign policy. A realist approach would not expect a state such as Poland to threaten international economic chaos; nor would it have expected private banks to have such autonomy. And, as would become apparent in the coming months, the amounts at stake in Poland were actually quite small, but they were sufficient to lock a variety of actors into a mutually dependent relationship.

Endnotes

[1]The "Group of Fifteen included Austria, Belgium, Britain, Canada, Denmark, Finland, France, Italy, Japan, Norway, the Netherlands, Sweden, Switzerland, the U.S., and West Germany.

[2]On U.S. sanctions against Poland see Stanislaw S. Wasowski, "U.S. Sanctions Against Poland", _Washington Quarterly_ 9 (Spring, 1986):167-184.

CHAPTER SEVEN

WALTZING WITH DISASTER:THE MEXICAN BAILOUT

For students of international debt the Mexican default scare of late 1982 is a required topic of investigation. While the threat to the international financial structure from a Polish default was real, it pales in comparison to the far-reaching implications of a halt in Mexico's debt service. A number of elements set the two situations apart.

As this chapter will show, the amount at risk to external creditors in Mexico was more than three times that in Poland. For many commercial banks, especially American ones, their exposure in Mexico represented a substantial portion of their total capital. A unilateral decision by Mexico, or a coordinated plan by Latin American debtors to halt debt service indefinitely, could have triggered an international panic of depositors wanting to withdraw funds far faster than banks could repay them.

Worsening the danger was the apparent speed with which the crisis approached. The lack of coordination among lenders meant that until late summer 1982 no outsider actually knew how dire Mexico's problems were. Largely for the same reason, no one knew exactly how much money was at stake in Mexico, or how many external creditors existed. Those authorities who could have known the magnitude of Mexico's external obligations, such as the banks and other western governments, either assumed that such lending would not have continued if it was not advisable, or that an American umbrella existed over Mexican debts. But the Reagan Administration for the most part still believed it should stay aloof from international finances.

One result of these factors is that when Mexican officials asked for assistance in staving off disaster, a real crisis existed. Mexico had hundreds of millions of dollars in debt payments due in a matter of days, with no way to cover the amounts by itself. Western decision makers in banks, MDBs, and state governments were forced to realize that other Latin American debtors such as Brazil and Argentina were experiencing similar problems. The fear of a default "contagion" became quite real as the Mexican bailout plan was arranged.

The rescue effort mounted for Mexico revealed that the U.S., and particularly the Reagan Administration, could respond to such a risk of economic turmoil, even if it did so only because it could see no alternative. It indicated that the debt management regime developed during the Polish rescheduling was intact and functioning, even if neither creditors nor debtors were content with the general situation. (There were no guarantees about its operating in the future, of course.) And the Mexican assistance effort helped to formalize what could be called a "rescue network" that by the middle of 1983 had rescheduled $44.9 billion owed by the so-called "ABM" (Argentina, Brazil, Mexico) debtor nations (Cline, 1984:31).[1]

The Mexican case is vital in attempting to understand international debt from a complex interdependence standpoint. The Mexican rescheduling involved a number of actors who were mutually dependent upon each other, though not necessarily to the same degree. Banks, creditor governments, MDBs, and even other debtor states could and did influence each other, both positively and negatively. No actor was able to act with impunity, because each was able to influence others. Mexico, for example, is an excellent example of a "weak" state which, as Keohane and Nye suggest, exercises its strength by manipulating the interdependence of other actors. In short, much of Keohane and Nye's model of world politics is reflected in the effort to reschedule Mexico's debt, including a changed definition of power, a reduction in the utility of force, the rise of non-security issues to the top of the international agenda, and a variety of shifts in the way actors' resources and goals turn into outcomes.

Historical Background

To understand even the basics of how Mexico developed its debt service problems in the 1980s, it is useful to start at the beginning of the previous decade.

In 1968, Luis Echeverria was the Minister of Interior during riots in Mexico City in which over one hundred students were killed by army troops. According to Kraft (1984:30), the event stimulated discussion in Mexico about the structure of the economy and its performance, especially for the poor and laboring classes. When Echeverria became President in 1970, he responded by replacing a number of orthodox government economists with radical reformers, and embarked upon an expansion of social programs. Funding was poured into education, health, and housing. To increase employment Echeverria stimulated tourism and industrial production. Mexico appeared ready to join the ranks of newly industrializing countries (NICs), and its annual growth rate reached 7% in 1971 and 1972.

But there were limits to this early boom. To pay for these expenditures, the dominant <u>Partido Revolucionario Institucional</u> (PRI) tried to raise taxes, but could not prevail against private sector opposition. The inflation rate, which had been fairly closely tied to that of the U.S., rose from 12% in 1973 to 24% in 1974, and held at 15% in 1975. The recession in developed states after the OPEC oil price increases of 1973 and 1974 reduced Mexican exports. Mexicans began to abandon the peso in favor of dollars. In August 1976 Mexico devalued the peso for the first time in twenty years, and was forced to work out an assistance package with the IMF.

The Mexican government looked to oil exports as a means to pay its bills (Kraft 1984:34-35). In 1974, hoping to benefit from the rise in oil prices, Mexico began an oil exploration drive. Proven oil and gas reserves increased ten-fold between 1976 and 1981. By the end of 1979 Mexico's crude oil exports allowed it to end the IMF program, and by 1980 "daily output was over 2 million barrels a day, half of it going for export, with receipts of about $80 billion" (Kraft, 1984:34). Mexico's economy was again expanding at a substantial pace. Growth rates averaged over 8% per year from 1978 to 1981 (Cline, 1982-1983:108), one-half million new jobs were created, and public and private investment increased 20% per year (Kraft, 1984:34).

But for the second time in less than a decade, Mexico's economic bubble burst, due to both domestic and foreign factors. Internally, the rapid rise in consumer demand outstripped the increase in goods available, and inflation ballooned in 1980. Again a run on the peso started, with consumers vacating their own currency in favor of U.S. dollars for purchases or investment across the northern border.

Externally, by 1981 developed countries had addressed the price increases of the second oil shock with reduced consumption and conservation. The oil market deteriorated dramatically (Cline, 1982-1983:108), and Mexico's prospects for increasing its revenue from oil exports disappeared. In June 1981 the head of Pemex, the nation's oil company, announced a decrease of premium crude oil prices from $30 to $28 per barrel, but with Mexico dependent upon oil for up to 75% of its export revenue opposition within President Lopez Portillo's cabinet prevented a decrease. With the price dropping elsewhere, by the fall oil exports had declined by one-fourth. By the time the price was finally reduced in September, Mexico had lost close to a billion dollars in export revenue. Coupled with the continuing run on the peso, Mexico endured a loss of at least $5 billion in foreign exchange for the year (Kraft, 1984:35). Mexico had been determined not to rely excessively on oil for export income (Riding, 1982a), but it experienced the same difficulty other developing states had in diversifying exports.

In many LDCs and NICs in the early 1980s, the combination of decreasing export revenues (due to slack demand in developed states), rising expenditures in domestic programs, and growing local consumer demand forced these nation-states to borrow from outside sources. Mexico was no different. External interests had been quite willing in

TABLE 12

MEXICO: ECONOMIC INDICATORS

(Billion dollars and percentages)

	1973	1974	1975	1976	1977	1978	1979	1980	1981	1982	1983
Exports	2.1	3.0	3.3	3.5	4.6	6.2	9.3	16.2	19.8	21.2	21.4
Imports	3.7	5.8	6.3	5.8	5.6	8.0	12.1	18.6	23.1	14.4	7.7
Current Account	-1.4	-2.9	-4.1	-3.4	-1.8	-3.2	-5.5	-7.9	-11.7	-4.9	5.5
Reserves	1.2	1.2	1.4	1.2	1.6	1.8	2.1	3.0	4.1	.8	3.9
Total Debt	8.6	12.8	16.9	21.8	27.1	33.6	40.8	53.8	74.1	84.1	86.7
Short-term debt	2.1	3.3	3.6	3.3	3.2	4.6	7.6	15.5	24.0	25.2	NA
Net debt/exports	154.6	182.0	243.8	286.5	309.7	278.2	241.7	205.7	242.4	272.7	308.0
Inflation	12.1	23.5	15.4	15.7	29.0	17.5	18.1	26.4	27.9	59.0	101.9

Source: IMF, International Financial Statistics, various issues; Inter-American Development Bank, Economic and Social Progress in Latin America, various years; BIS, Maturity Distribution of International Bank Lending, various years; CEPAL, Balance Preliminar 1983; Banco de Mexico Informe Anual 1983; Solis and Zedillo, "A Few Considerations on the Foreign Debt of Mexico," 1984; and Institute for International Economics debt data base. Cited in Cline, 1984:258-259.

Note: Merchandise exports and imports. Nongold reserves. Net debt as percentage of exports of goods and services. Consumer price inflation, year over year.

the past to lend Mexico money. (See Table 12). Mexico's oil wealth had seemed to guarantee rapid growth in the middle and late 1970s, and its close trading relationship with the U.S. caused creditors to see the U.S. as a guarantor of Mexico's economic health and loans to it. For American banks especially, the upheaval in Iran in 1979, the usual turmoil of Middle East politics, and the willingness of Latin American states to borrow stimulated lending in the western hemisphere.

Consequently, Mexico's external debt rose dramatically in the early 1980s. For example, in 1981 Pemex tripled its total debt when it borrowed $10 billion. For the entire year Mexico's external debt grew at least $20 billion from the previous year's total. And while Mexico needed to borrow, U.S. banks were especially talented at finding ways to avoid legal proscriptions on lending beyond a particular amount (Kraft, 1984:20):

> Another problem grew out of the rules applied by federal and state authorities to limit the amount a bank can loan to a single customer. A "means and purpose" test allows banks to list loans to different government entities separately provided each entity has an independent financial base. But the Mexicans came into the market with so many different governmental corporations that the financial base was difficult to distinguish. There was the government itself, technically, the United Mexican States. Then there was the national oil company, Pemex. Then the Development Bank, Nafinsa. Then the Telephone Company, and the nationalized steel plant, and the fisheries, and sugar mills and so forth. In the end, the banks came to loan to the Mexican government in more than a score of different guises.

What exacerbated matters was the fact that by 1980 some banks had begun worrying about the debt "overhang" in Latin America, and started to reduce long-term loan packages. With banks taking the lead from each other, the problem was compounded (Cohen, 1985:142). According to Kraft, at the beginning of 1981 only 5% of Mexico's loans were due within twelve months; by year's end that figure was 22%. Maturities first dropped to six months, then lower, with the bulk of repayment due dates grouped in two periods, in February and August (1984:35). Kuczynski (1988:79) reports that between the end of 1979 and the end of 1981, $17 billion of Mexico's $26 billion increase in bank debt was in the form of short term loans.[2]

So by early 1982, most of what could have gone wrong for Mexico had. Overall exports were increasing slightly, but the value of Mexico's main export was dropping. And imports were rising also. Public sector spending was increasing, fueled by the perceptions of 1979 and 1980 that oil revenues could balance the budget. Government expenditures resulted in a large budget deficit. Foreign lenders were little help, and rising interest rates made external borrowing at best a very painful method of addressing the gathering crisis (Kuczynski, 1988:74):

> Between 1979 and 1981, the years of peak export growth because of high oil prices, [Mexico's] external debt to banks nearly doubled. With an external debt by 1981 equivalent to three times exports, an interest rate of 10 percent would have required 30 percent of exports just to pay the interest on the debt. But for 1981 the average interest on the debt had risen to about 17 percent, so that 51 percent of export earnings were required to cover interest. The stage for the crisis was then set because the debtor--other things being equal--would need to raise its borrowing abroad by two-thirds in the short space of a year or so in order to pay interest without disrupting its economy. When that became impossible, the crisis arrived.

While the full magnitude of its difficulties may not have been obvious, by the middle of 1982 it was clear that Mexico--along with much of Latin America--was in financial trouble (Cohen, 1985:142-143). Mexico's interest burden for 1982 alone was estimated at $12 billion (Riding,1982b:D13), an increase from $5.4 billion in 1980 and $8.2 billion in 1981 (Cline, 1984:258). At the end of April, June, and July the U.S. Federal Reserve organized twenty-four hour currency swaps so that Mexico could report adherence to its legal month-end currency reserve requirements. It arranged another trade of $700 million in early August on the understanding Mexico would use the funds to apply for a bridge loan from the IMF (Kraft, 1984:8). In June Mexico raised $2.5 billion in the Eurocurrency market (Cohen, 1985:142), but not without serious problems, even though the interest rates were a full point above those on previous Mexican packages. A month and a half later Mexico received another $100 million loan, this one at 18.5% interest, and arranged by Merrill Lynch. This would be the last loan before Mexico formally asked for assistance (Kraft, 1984:37).

What may have pushed Mexico over the financial precipice were well-intentioned government austerity measures (Cline, 1984:259). After resounding success for the PRI in the July 1982 national elections, Lopez Portillo's administration imposed price increases of 100% on bread and tortillas and of 50% on gasoline. The goal was to reduce expensive government subsidies in the long run, but for the short term the result was highly inflationary. The Mexican public moved to convert pesos into dollars, fueling capital flight that cost Mexico almost $9 billion in the first nine months of 1982. With foreign exchange reserves falling rapidly, the government mandated that domestic dollar deposits could only be redeemable in pesos, imposed a dual exchange rate, and temporarily closed exchange markets. When the market did reopen the peso fell from 70 to 120 per dollar.

On Thursday, August 12, Mexico's Finance Minister Jesus Silva Herzog telephoned Washington, D.C. He spoke with Federal Reserve Chair

Paul Volcker, Treasure Secretary Donald Regan, and IMF Managing Director Jacques de Larosiére. He told each that Mexico would no longer be able to service its debt without assistance, and that he would be in the U.S. capitol the next day to discuss the matter.

The Bailout Scramble

Silva's telephone call set off a wild scramble by various actors that would eventually stretch over the next four months[3]. At virtually any time Mexico could have been declared in default of its obligations. There was quite literally no way to know what the implications would be if that happened, but the actors unanimously sought other outcomes. The effort to avoid such a possibility therefore required a tightrope act by a number of actors with differing goals and understandings of the international political economy.

The First Weekend

Silva flew to Washington Thursday night, August 12, along with Angel Gurria, the director of Mexico's Department of Public Credit, central bank director Miguel Mancera, and Mancera's deputy Alfredo Phillips Olmedo (Kuczynski, 1988:82-83). The next morning Silva's first stop was at the IMF, to meet with de Larosiére.

Silva told the IMF director that Mexico had immediate and severe debt service problems and wished to apply for the maximum IMF loan for which it was eligible. He indicated President Lopez Portillo was willing to negotiate an austerity program for Mexico. Silva acknowledged the need for early IMF approval as a way of encouraging banks and official creditors to postpone debt payments.

De Larosiére indicated his willingness to help, but warned Silva it would take a number of weeks for the IMF's governors to approval any loan package. He also insisted on three conditions for further discussions. First, because of Lopez Portillo's long-standing dislike of the IMF, de Larosiére requested the Mexican government publicly announce its application for Fund assistance. Second, he reiterated the Fund's opposition to excessive market regulation, because Mexico had recently imposed exchange controls. Finally, the director suggested Silva coordinate all relief efforts in one package involving the Fund, banks, and creditor governments (Kraft, 1984:6-7).

After Silva left, de Larosiére met with staff members and began estimating just how much money Mexico would need. That evening, the director met with Federal Reserve chair Paul Volcker, whom he informed it would take the Fund six weeks to arrange an IMF package for Mexico. Three days later a trio of IMF officials went to Mexico City to begin studying Mexico's finances.

Silva's next visit that Friday, August 13 was with Volcker. The Federal Reserve chair had plenty of reason to be concerned about Mexico's plight. For the previous three years the Fed's tight money policy had virtually eradicated inflation in the U.S., but it had also left the American economy in a deep recession. Only in recent months had the Fed began to ease monetary expansion, and recovery was slow. Volcker believed that with the degree of American bank exposure there a Mexican default would be catastrophic for the U.S. Mexico's problems were not especially surprising to Volcker; he and his assistants had kept a close watch on the Mexican economy for some time, and after Silva had become finance minister in March 1982 the two talked often of Mexico's situation and Lopez Portillo's reluctance to try the IMF cure.

Silva gave Volcker his assessment of conditions, and reported his request to the IMF for a relief package. Silva said Mexico needed American help in making $3 billion in debt payments due in August and September (Makin, 1984:13). In fact, Silva indicated some assistance was required immediately, that weekend in fact, because of payments coming due in three days. The finance minister also told the Federal Reserve chair of his nation's need for enough funds from the Fed and other central banks to keep Mexico solvent until the IMF program could be arranged and the debt to private banks rescheduled.

Volcker immediately recognized that the greatest danger to the international economic system was the possibility that commercial banks, especially American ones, would declare a default on Mexico's debts. Other concerns, such as Mexico's role as the third largest importer of American goods (see Hartland-Thunberg and Ebinger, 1986), were minor in comparison. Money center banks had survived two default scares in the last year: the Polish one, and the Argentine one after the Falklands war. Mexico's external debt was far larger than the others' (roughly $80 billion outstanding, in comparison with $25 billion owed by Poland and $37 billion by Argentina), and the amount of U.S. bank capital exposed there was tremendous. (See Table 13.) A Mexican default would invite the same elsewhere in Latin America. Volcker decided the U.S. would have to find a way for Mexico to continue to service its debt to banks, to avoid a chance that one bank could call a default and in so doing induce others to do the same (Kraft, 1984:9-10).

So Volcker pressed Silva to arrange a meeting as soon as possible with the major commercial lenders. He even supplied Silva with a list of telephone numbers where, as Kraft writes "even on vacation in the depth of an August week-end, the leading American bankers could be reached" (1984:9). Before leaving Washington Sunday night, Silva contacted the heads of seven of the U.S.'s largest banks, and began work creating an advisory committee to deal with the situation.

Volcker also learned from Silva that a $700 million currency swap the Fed had made with Mexico on August 4, which the U.S. had expected to help Mexico remain solvent through September, had already been used. An

IMF package would provide some relief, but it would not be forthcoming for weeks. Such was also the case for bank rescheduling. In the interim, Mexico needed several billion dollars just to stay current on its interest payments. Volcker told Silva $1.5 billion might be arranged from central banks, and that the U.S. could perhaps supply half

TABLE 13

EXPOSURE AS PERCENTAGE OF CAPITAL, END 1982
(U.S. Banks with at least $1 billion exposed)

	Argentina	Brazil	Mexico	Venezuela	Chile	Total	Capital[a] (million dollars)
Citibank	18.2	73.5	54.6	18.2	10.0	174.5	5,989
Bank of America	10.2	47.9	52.1	41.7	6.3	158.2	4,799
Chase Manhattan	21.3	56.9	40.0	24.0	11.8	154.0	4,221
Morgan Guarantee	24.4	54.3	34.8	17.5	9.7	140.7	3,107
Manufacturers Hanover	47.5	77.7	66.7	42.4	28.4	262.8	2,592
Chemical	14.9	52.0	60.0	28.0	14.8	169.7	2,499
Continental Illinois	17.8	22.9	32.4	21.6	12.8	107.5	2,143
Bankers Trust	13.2	46.2	46.2	25.1	10.6	141.2	1,895
First National Chicago	14.5	40.6	50.1	17.4	11.6	134.2	1,725
Security Pacific	10.4	29.1	31.2	4.5	7.4	82.5	1,684
Wells Fargo	8.3	40.7	51.0	20.4	6.2	26.6	1,201
Crocker National	38.1	57.3	51.2	22.8	26.5	196.0	1,080
First Interstate	6.9	43.9	63.0	18.5	3.7	136.0	1,080

TABLE 13 - Continued

Marine Midland	NA	47.8	28.3	29.2	NA	NA	1,074
Mellon	NA	35.3	41.1	17.6	NA	NA	1,024

Source: Cline, 1984, p. 24

NA--Not Available

aincludes shareholders equity, subordinated notes, and reserves against possible loan losses.

the amount. The Federal Reserve chair suggested a Bank for International Settlements meeting was in order, and by the end of the weekend Volcker had talked by telephone with central bank officials in Britain, Canada, France, West Germany, Japan, and Switzerland. A BIS meeting was quickly scheduled for August 18 in Basel, Switzerland.

While Silva's visits with de Larosiére and Volcker allowed him to indicate the gravity of the situation, and moved the two officials to act, the finance minister had not actually received any funds yet. On Friday afternoon he met with Treasury Secretary Regan (Kraft, 1984:10-11). Treasury officials had been aware of some of Mexico's financial problems, and a month earlier had explored with other government departments the possibility of making advance purchases of Mexican oil to help if a financial emergency arose. Yet even with some notice, the Treasury staff was surprised at the rapid turn of events, and a crisis atmosphere began to pervade the negotiations.

By the time of Silva's arrival at the Treasury Department early Friday afternoon, Regan had assigned Deputy Treasury Secretary R.T. McNamar to handle negotiations. The Americans laid out a "remarkably accurate" (Kraft, 1984:13) estimate of Mexico's debt position. It revealed that Mexico had less than $200 million in reserves available. With at least $100 million being lost each day, Mexico could be in default in less than three days. A deal would have to be reached and publicized before banks opened on Monday to avoid the risk of a default call.

Talks between the Mexicans and Treasury officials proceeded all afternoon and into the evening. By the end of the day, Gurria and his American counterparts determined what amounts Mexico owed, to whom, and when they were due. It was also decided that the Treasury Department would organize $2 billion of U.S. government assistance as part of a $3.5 billion relief package needed before the IMF could act. That part of the discussions was rather simple. The difficult portion was in determining in what form the relief would be arranged.

A decision was made that part of the package would be in the form of food credits. A number of previous U.S. assistance efforts to Mexico had involved such measures. Treasury officials ascertained there were surplus agricultural products which Mexico could purchase. During a jog together Saturday morning, McNamar convinced Agriculture Department Secretary John Block to extend $1 billion in Commodity Credit Corporation (CCC) credits to Mexico ("Billions", 1982:D1). This would not result in funds being sent directly to Mexico, but it would free $1 billion in purchasing power which could be used for loan payments.

As for the other $1 billion in U.S. assistance, both sides had been contemplating a U.S. purchase of Mexican oil. On Friday afternoon negotiators determined from the Energy Department that the U.S. could utilize the type of crude Mexico had available, and that the Strategic Petroleum Reserve (SPR), under the control of the Defense Department, had $1 billion available for the purchase. Finally, the approval of the Office of Management and Budget (OMB) was required for the Treasury's Exchange Stabilization Fund to advance $1 billion against a $1 billion payment due from the SPR within five days. The OMB would only approve the deal if the purchase could be justified to Congress as an advantageous use of federal funds. This would require a good deal for the U.S., and almost certainly an unpleasant one for Mexico (Kraft, 1984:14).

The entire relief effort very nearly came apart on this issue. The original U.S. goal was to purchase oil at about $4 per barrel under the prevailing global price (approximately $32 per barrel). Silva was immediately reluctant. First, setting an official price on oil in the relief package could alienate Mexico from other global producers who would dislike being undersold. Second, Silva knew the prospect of selling oil to the U.S. at bargain prices would anger many Mexicans. Instead of acting unilaterally, Silva called Lopez Portillo, who promptly sent his Minister of Patrimony, Jose Andres Oteyza, and the Director of Pemex, Julio Rudolfo Moctezuma Cid, to Washington.

Oteyza refused to approve any deal denominating a dollar per barrel price (Kraft, 1984:14-15). A proposal was then advanced for a $1 billion U.S. loan to Mexico against repayment in oil; this loan would carry interest charges. Late Saturday U.S. negotiators suggested that in exchange for a $1 billion loan Mexico pay back $1.3 billion in oil over the next fifteen months. This amounted to a 35% interest bill, and Oteyza called Lopez Portillo to consult. The President insisted Mexico would pay nothing over 20%, and ordered negotiations halted. When talks ended Saturday night the very real possibility of a Mexican default was less than forty-eight hours away.

On Sunday morning, August 15, American negotiators met at the Treasury Department and suggested imposing a $100 million negotiating fee, in place of the thinly disguised interest charges on the oil deal. McNamar and U.S. Ambassador to Mexico John Gavin pitched the idea to

Oteyza and Silva in the Mexican's Watergate hotel suite. The idea of a fee was acceptable to Oteyza and Silva, but not the $100 million amount. Silva telephoned his president again, who again instructed his officials to halt discussions. Silva told Gavin and McNamar he would have lunch at the Mexican Embassy, and then leave for home (Kraft, 1984:15).

Gavin and McNamar hurried back to the Treasury Department to meet with other U.S. officials. Their suggestion to Silva of a reduced fee had met with some interest, and they argued for a reduction in the negotiating fee to $50 million. The OMB firmly opposed any reduction. With Silva and the other Mexican officials practically on a plane for home, Treasury Secretary Regan reentered the discussions.

Regan had been out of town Saturday, and Sunday morning flew by helicopter to Camp David to see President Reagan. The President indicated to Regan he wanted American help for Mexico if at all possible. Regan flew back to the Treasury, and McNamar and Gavin reported the progress--or lack thereof--in the negotiations. Regan said that he would take responsibility for ordering the OMB to approve the deal.

McNamar then reached Silva and Oteyza at the Mexican Embassy, and asked them to return for further talks. The Mexicans called Lopez Portillo again, who gave them permission to continue negotiations. From late in the afternoon until well into that evening, Mexican and American officials met at the Treasury and hammered out the particulars on the arrangement that would keep Mexico solvent until the IMF and central and commercial banks could also arrange relief packages.

The final arrangement reflected the number of different U.S. agencies which were involved in the effort. The U.S. gave Mexico $1 billion against the purchase of Mexican oil for the Strategic Petroleum Reserve. Mexico agreed to increase its crude deliveries to the U.S. from 50,000 to 190,000 barrels per day ("Billions, 1982:D5). The Commodity Credit Corporation extended $1 billion in credits for the purchase of American farm commodities. The Federal Reserve agreed to supply at least $750 million as part of a BIS bridge loan; the amount could be greater as Fed chief Volcker was committed to matching whatever other central banks contributed (Makin, 1984:13; Kuczynski, 1988:87). And most importantly, the U.S. government committed itself to trying to enforce an unofficial payments delay by U.S. banks, until a formal rescheduling agreement could be worked out.

The BIS Comes Aboard

On Wednesday, August 18, three days after the U.S. assistance package for Mexico was completed, central bank officials from around the world met at the Bank of International Settlements in Basel. Federal Reserve Chair Paul Volcker had telephoned the heads of various central banks the past weekend; this emergency meeting was the result. The BIS had held its last regular meeting in July, and officials were not scheduled for another one until September. But at the prompting of Volcker--and events--a group of subordinate officials of the G-10 countries[4] known as the Eurocurrency Standing Committee met to discuss Mexico's need for debt relief (Kraft, 1984:18-19).

In his telephone conversations Volcker had already obtained general agreement on the need for a $1.5 billion loan to Mexico, of which the U.S. would supply half. He was convinced the other central banks would participate. Volcker reasoned that while American banks had the greatest exposure in Mexico, and more generally in Latin America, other central banks could not ignore the possibility of a debt structure "meltdown". The British, for example, with London as a major financial center, had a sizable stake in the stability of the global financial system. And many other countries had official and private debts due from Eastern Europe on which they wanted American support.

The BIS negotiations, as usual, were rapidly completed. Before adjourning later that same day, the Eurocurrency Standing Committee gave its tentative approval, pending the formal agreement by the G-10 governors, for a bridge loan to keep Mexico operating until an IMF package could be completed. The bankers agreed to match the U.S. commitment of $750 million, and when Spain added $175 million the U.S. matched that as well, finalizing a package of $1.85 billion (Kuczynski, 1988:87).

The Second Weekend

The IMF was moving toward an assistance package, and the U.S. government and the central banks were committed to providing funds to cover any immediate debts. But still to be dealt with were the commercial banks that held the majority of Mexican debt, and which could still declare a default. So shortly after the BIS meeting ended on August 18, Silva Herzog flew from Mexico City to New York to meet commercial bankers.

The next day Silva met with many of the bank officials he had contacted during the previous weekend (Kraft, 1984:19-21). With Volcker's assistance an advisory committee of banks had been set up to deal with the most pressing of Mexico's debt payment problems, and to serve as liaisons between Mexico and its hundreds of smaller creditor banks. Representatives of the advisory committee banks helped contact other banks, and called them to a meeting on Friday, August 20 at the Federal Reserve Bank of New York. Early Friday morning Silva and the advisory group held a practice question-and-answer session, attempting to anticipate the type of inquiries Silva was likely to hear from bankers.

Estimates of the number of commercial banks to which Mexico owed money ran as high as one thousand (Kuczynski, 1988:88). Officials of approximately eight hundred were invited to the meeting, and 115 sent representatives. At the Friday meeting the chief of the New York Federal Reserve bank, Anthony Solomon, introduced the discussion by summarizing the results of the past weekend's talks and the BIS's relief package. He told the assembly that while the Federal Reserve had supplied the meeting place, any arrangement would have to be made by Mexico and its creditor banks. Nonetheless, Solomon pointed to the recent official negotiations as evidence that various governments strongly wanted some cooperation among the other parties.

Silva addressed the bankers next. Publically he put the best face possible on Mexico's position, which privately he knew was worsening. Originally the minister intended to ask for a postponement until the end of the year on Mexico's bank debts. His previous discussions with the advisory committee convinced him to ask for a ninety day moratorium (Cowan, 1982:A32). Silva told the bankers of Mexico's intention to develop an adjustment program with the IMF, and that austerity measures would help redress his country's balance of payments deficit. He announced Mexico would continue to service its interest payments, but would need the ninety day delay in principal due.

After he concluded, Silva took questions from the audience. Mixed in with queries about how Mexico intended to dig itself out of its problems were indications of support from the largest banks, which had the most to lose. While smaller banks were less sanguine in their tone, it was quickly becoming apparent that they were not going to have an equal voice with money center banks in determining how Mexico's debt would be handled. As Kraft reports, "At the end, Silva put out a press release. It claimed that all the commercial banks had 'accepted in principle the Mexican proposal of rolling over the maturities...' Several of them present later complained that they had not said no. But, as a practical matter, the commercial banks, too, had been hooked." (1984:22). That afternoon, the advisory committee began work in what was shaping up as a second crisis weekend (Kuczynski, 1988:88). Representatives of major international banks[5] met at Citibank's New York offices. Citibank, Bank of America, and Swiss Bank Corporation were designated co-chairs of the committee. The committee's first business involved alerting Mexico's creditor banks to the advisory committee's activities so that an agreement on rescheduling Mexico's loans could be pursued. That required ascertaining exactly how much Mexico owed, to whom, and when the amounts were due. Angel Gurria, the director of Mexico's Department of Public Credit, was recalled from Newark airport where he was preparing to leave for Mexico. Another set of meetings, fully as important as the ones in Washington the previous weekend, began.

The advisory committee and Mexican officials spent much of the weekend contacting banks to request they rollover Mexican debts coming due within the next few weeks. On Sunday August 22 the discussants also sent out two telexes. The first, from Silva, detailed Mexico's desire to deal with its debt problems, and the efforts by the IMF, the BIS, and the U.S. to keep Mexico solvent. It also confirmed the existence of an advisory committee, and that Mexican officials had met with bankers two days before; it closed with the request for a postponement of principal due in the ninety days after August 23. The second telex was sent by the committee itself, and stated Mexico's proposal for a payments moratorium was part of a widely supported package of initiatives designed to return Mexico to financial health. The committee indicated it supported Mexico's request, and considered "its acceptance by all banks to be essential" (Kraft, 1984:25) if time was to be found for rescheduling. By the end of the weekend the negotiators in New York had done virtually all they could to prevent a Mexican default.

The IMF Mission

On August 16, only four days after Silva's telephone calls to Washington, a group of IMF negotiators went to Mexico City. Their first task was to determine just how much relief Mexico would need, because there was little exact information available about the size and distribution of Mexico's obligations. The team eventually estimated the country's outstanding external debt at $81 billion, $67.5 billion of which was owed to commercial banks (Makin, 1984:12). The team's second responsibility was to develop a set of austerity measures for Mexico which would cause the IMF's governors to approve an assistance package. The IMF mission set up operations at the Bank of Mexico where its members worked closely with a team of officials from Mexico's finance ministry and central bank.

Negotiations proceeded rather quickly, and an early agreement seemed possible. By the weekend of August 28 and 29 virtually the entire arrangement was complete, including provisions for a severe cut in Mexico's federal budget deficit and other adjustment measures. Both sides believed the package could be finished at the IMF/World Bank's joint annual meeting in Toronto starting September 5. But one more obstacle was about to be placed on the road to rescheduling.

Throughout much of 1982 President Lopez Portillo had vacillated between two very different approaches to his nation's economic problems. On the one side were options favored by more radical members of his administration. These included exchange restrictions, national control of the banks, and even outright repudiation of Mexico's external debt. On the opposing side were more economically and politically conservative measures; these included the effort the finance minister was making to arrange another IMF plan similar to the one used in 1976. Even as Silva began negotiations in Washington, however, Lopez Portillo remained hopeful another option existed (Kraft, 1984:38):

For the next two weeks--as Silva moved forward with the American government, the IMF, and the BIS--Lopez Portillo hung in the background. But all year long, he had been considering an alternate course urged on him by the radical economists in his entourage. The radicals found the root of trouble in the disposition of Mexico's banks and rich middle class to move money out of the country. That could be stopped, it was asserted, by nationalization of the banks, and the imposition of exchange controls. The funds locked in Mexico could then be channeled by government into productive investments. With no need to compete against U.S. money markets, interest rates could be lowered, making it attractive for Mexicans to buy on credit, and for businessmen to invest in new facilities. Silva and [Director Miguel] Mancera of the central bank had opposed this view on the inside and on the outside. Mancera, indeed, published a pamphlet--Inconveniencia del Control de Cambios, or The Disadvantages of Exchange Controls-- showing that such measures could not be made to work because of the multifold connections linking Mexico with the U.S. "Rather than stemming the flight of capital," Mancera wrote of controls, they "would actually multiply it due to the loss of confidence that would be caused by establishment of controls." Still, as the time for actually swallowing the IMF medicine drew nigh, Lopez Portillo hesitated.

On August 31 Lopez Portillo decided on the radical approach, and signed two orders (Cline, 1982-1983:109). The first nationalized the banks. The second imposed exchange controls. The next day, he revealed his decision in a speech to Parliament. He argued his initiatives would increase investment in oil production, create jobs, stimulate growth, provide more funds for social programs, and allow a more active foreign policy.

No one was exactly certain what Lopez Portillo's actions meant for the IMF negotiations, but it was clearly not good news. Genuine fear over the future gripped some of the parties gathering in Toronto for the IMF meeting. Lopez Portillo was threatening to discard the entire IMF program which had been close to completion. Reports were heard that almost half of Mexico's army had been brought to the capital to prevent riots ("Threat", 1982:106). It seemed possible a coup d'état could prevent president-elect Miguel de la Madrid Hurtado from surviving until his scheduled inauguration on December 1. As Walter Wriston of Citibank later described the mood in Toronto, "We had 150-odd finance ministers, 50-odd central bankers, 1000 journalists, 1000 commercial bankers, a large supply of whiskey and a reasonably small city that produced an enormous head of steam driving the engine called 'the end of the world is coming'" (quoted in Kraft, 1984:40).

Officials in Toronto found themselves having to mount two fresh rescue operations. The first involved payments which Mexican branch banks owed to other banks. Since the August 20 meeting with private bankers Mexico had been committed to remaining current with these payments, but most banks held off on calling these debts because of the pending rescheduling effort. The implications of Lopez Portillo's actions began to influence the debt market, and it became clear no quick fix was to be arranged in Toronto. On Tuesday, September 7 (the previous day was a holiday) Mexican branch banks in New York were overwhelmed with demands by other banks for payment of loans and deposits. At the close of business the Mexican banks were $70 million short. Federal Reserve Chair Volcker was contacted; he consulted with Silva. Late that day the Federal Reserve deposited $70 million from the BIS funds advanced to Mexico in the accounts of American banks which had temporarily covered the shortfall. Soon the Fed and other central banks were pressuring Mexico to force Mexican branch banks to ignore demands for repayment unless legal action was imminent. It seemed the entire U.S. and BIS assistance packages could disappear through the interbank market in a matter of weeks. Disaster was avoided as the interbank market was calmed, but a thinly disguised crisis atmosphere lasted for two months.

The second operation at Toronto involved restarting the negotiations between the IMF and Mexico. Silva contacted de Larosiére and asked for a set of conditions the finance minister could take to his president which would convince him to allow talks to proceed. The IMF team which had been at work in Mexico assembled in Toronto, and drafted a letter which mentioned in guarded terms the IMF's free market commitments, but was phrased not to offend Lopez Portillo. Silva returned to Mexico, and with options almost nonexistent for both sides received the president's approval for further negotiations.

As events would have it, the IMF package which was nearly complete before September 1 took another two months to finalize. With the ninety-day moratorium on bank principal due to expire in less than two weeks, on November 10 the particulars of the IMF deal were announced. In exchange for almost $3.9 billion in IMF funds (which would hopefully instigate banks to reschedule Mexico's debts), Mexico would adopt adjustment measures (Cline, 1982-1983:110). The country's federal budget deficit would be reduced from 16.5% of GNP in 1981 to 8.5% in 1983, to 5.5% in 1984, and to 3.5% in 1985 (Riding, 1982d:D3). External debt would increase in 1983 a maximum of $5 billion, and inflation would be cut almost in half. Restrictive policies would be imposed in nearly every sector of the Mexican economy.

Bailing In the Banks

Still Mexico would not receive any IMF funds until de Larosiére formally presented the signed Letter of Intent to the IMF's governors. By all accounts, it was at this point that the managing director decided to force the banks, which were at least partly responsible for Mexico's woes, to provide a share of assistance. After working with Volcker and other central bank officials de Larosiére called the chairs and chief executives of thirteen money center banks to a meeting at the New York Fed on November 16. It was there he announced the banks would only be "bailed out" if they were "bailed in".

The director spelled out to the bankers the terms of the letter of intent which had been finalized, and summarized Mexico's financial position (Kraft, 1984:48-49). He indicated in 1983 Mexico would need $1.5 billion for reserves and another $2.55 billion to cover loans from the Fed and the BIS. Assuming a deficit of over $4 billion, that meant Mexico would need more than $8 billion. The IMF was prepared to loan a substantial amount, de Larosiére said, and he believed $2 billion could come from the U.S. and other countries. But he insisted the banks contribute $5 billion in new loans ("IMF Orders", 1982:34-35).

And de Larosiére made it clear it was not a request (Kuczynski, 1988:89-90). Unless the banks produced the funds, he would refuse to recommend to the IMF's governors that the organization fund the Mexican bailout package. With the board scheduled to meet December 23, de Larosiére announced he would expect to have a bank package arranged by December 15.

When the shock to the bankers abated, it was clear that the world of international finance had undergone a major change, and the term "forced lending" had come to have real meaning. Events had brought forth the fact that no actor interested in Mexico's debt could act with impunity, or in isolation. If the banks were going to play brinkmanship with the rescheduling of Mexico's debt, as they had the previous year with Poland, de Larosiére and his allies in the central banks were prepared to play as well.

The banks--especially the largest ones--were moved to action by de Larosiére and by Volcker's remarks in a speech that night that indicated the Fed would relax supervision of loans made to assist Mexico (Cohen, 1985:143-144). The next day the advisory committee met. It approved Mexico's request for another ninety-day extension on principal payments; the old extension had been scheduled to expire in six days. On November 30 the committee decided to raise the required funds by assessing all of Mexico's creditor banks an additional 7% contribution to the new package. On December 1 Miguel de la Madrid took office as Mexico's new president. Silva continued as finance minister, and his colleague Carlos Salinas de Gortari took over as minister of budget and programming. The apparent calming of events in Mexico encouraged bankers to negotiate seriously.

On December 8 a deal on bank debt was completed (Kraft, 1984:51). The agreement entailed $5 billion in new loans, to be repaid over six years after a three year grace period; the interest rate was set at 2.25% over LIBOR. A negotiating fee of 1.25% was charged at the outset. The amount rescheduled totaled $20 billion, and the payments moratorium on it was extended through 1984. After that there would be a four year grace period, with repayment then over eight years. A one percent negotiating fee was imposed, along with an interest rate of 1.875% over LIBOR.

For a final time defeat could yet be snatched from the jaws of victory. Despite the excellent rates of interest the advisory committee got on the new package, participation by Mexico's creditor banks was not unanimous. Many small and regional banks in the U.S., and entire banking systems in other countries, were reluctant to provide any more

TABLE 14

FINANCIAL RESCUE PACKAGES TO MID-1983
(Aid to Argentina, Brazil, Mexico, and Yugoslavia
in billion dollars)

	Argentina	Brazil	Mexico	Yugoslavia
Financial Support				
IMF				
Stand-by	1.7	---	---	0.6
Extended Fund Facility	---	4.6	3.7	---
Compensatory finance and other	0.5	1.3	0.22	---
World Bank	---	---	---	0.5
BIS	0.5	1.2	0.925	0.5
United States				
Oil payments	---	---	1.0	---
Commodity Credit	---	---	1.0	0.2
Federal Reserve	---	0.4	0.925	---
Treasury	---	1.53	---	---
Private banks, new loans	1.5	4.4	5.0	3.0[a]
Government trade credits	---	---	2.0	1.1
Total	4.25	13.4	14.7	5.9

TABLE 14 - Continued

Debt Rescheduling

Amount[b]	5.5	4.9	19.5[c]	NA
Originally due	1982-83	long-term 1983	8/82-12/84	NA

Source: Cline, 1984, p. 31.

[a]$600 million in new loans; $1.2 billion to repay matured debt; $1.2 billion stretch-out of short-term loans.

[b]Public debt.

[c]Other arrangements effectively rescheduled $15 billion in private debt.

funds. Advisory committee banks pressured their smaller colleagues to come aboard, and the U.S. Treasury contacted counterpart ministries in other countries to request pressure on local banks. An entire network of central and private bank officials spent the week after the December 8 agreement trying to find $5 billion in new funds.

On December 22 de Larosiére received the commitment of export agencies in Britain, France, Germany, Japan, and the U.S. for $2 billion in new government funds he requested. The next day he went to the IMF board with the commitment of $4.3 billion in new bank loans which he termed a sufficient "critical mass" to bail in the banks. With these two steps the last group of actors came aboard the assistance effort. Two days before Christmas the IMF formally agreed to muster a loan package of $3.9 billion for Mexico (Farnsworth, 1982f).

Conclusions

The effort to "rescue" Mexico suggests a number of conclusions about the international debt issue area, and how the politics of debt are explained within international relations theory. One obvious lesson is that the Mexican default scare reflects how little control over events and outcomes decision makers have:

> The rush to get the Mexican default out of the way came at a price. In the short term there was a significant financial cost; but more important, in the long term there was at least a possibility that the containment strategy might not be viable. Was there a practical alternative? At the time the facts of the situation

probably precluded a slower and more deliberate approach. Mexico alone accounted for perhaps 10 percent of all Euromarket placement of funds and for a higher proportion of medium term lending. These loans had been placed among a far larger number of banks than for any other borrower; five large U.S. banks had close to the whole of their capital tied up in loans to Mexico. The potential for a major international financial crisis, especially coming at the end of a deep international recession and after record high interest rates, was certainly there (Kuczynski, 1988:90).

Mexico's financial problems justifiably raised international debt on the agenda of global concerns. The total amount at risk in Mexico in late 1982 was more than three times that exposed in Poland in 1981. Not only was the risk greater for Mexico's future, but the danger of financial collapse was spread more widely among a variety of actors. No one was willing to predict that a default in Mexico would not have stimulated similar turns of events elsewhere, through the impetus of either creditors or debtors. If banks had refused to rollover old loans, and make new ones, the "default option" could well have meant the global equivalent of depression-era bank runs. No western government could have come close to guaranteeing all the funds depositors might seek to withdraw.

Overall, a great deal of luck was involved in the Mexican rescue. It is perhaps accurate to describe the four-month process as similar to having a number of individuals locked in a dark room, where each is handed a pistol that shoots both forward and backward at the same time. Each knows that he may be able to harm the others, and certainly knows a lot of shooting is likely if he fires, but in the darkness he is unable to know just how badly he will hurt his own cause in the process. Kuczynski (1988:90-91) notes as crucial the presence of certain very perceptive and patient individuals. They included Volcker, de Larosiére, and McNamar, and William Rhodes, the well-connected Citibank executive who chaired the advisory committee. And without any doubt the entire effort would have collapsed without the exertions of Silva, who navigated a difficult path among the conflicting approaches and demands of all the other actors. It was also fortunate that these individuals had much in common in the ways and places they were trained, in the language--linguistically and professionally--which they spoke, and in their conceptions of global economics (see Astiz, 1983; Samuels, 1986). These factors made the creation of a "rescue network", while tortuous, much simpler.

The Mexican default scare had two broader results, beyond merely indicating the importance of strategically placed individuals. The first has already been touched upon: the formalizing of a "rescue network" for assisting sovereign debtors. As Table 14 indicates, in the months after the Mexican bailout the same actors coordinated efforts on the other "ABM" countries and Yugoslavia as well (see also Fishlow, 1986:88-89; Cohen, 1985:143). The second result was the movement of the

Reagan Administration to action. With the completion of a clear lesson in the inability of the global capitalist system to govern itself, a small but vital group within the Administration began to rethink the Reagan view of the world economy and of its actors and processes. (See Chapters Eight and Nine).

Finally, the Mexican case provides a strong indication of the existence of complex interdependence within the international debt issue area. This is made most obvious by the existence of a number of mutually dependent actors, all of whom possessed limited capabilities to dictate the actions of others.

As for the characteristics of complex interdependence, there were indeed multiple channels of contact. Involved were banks, the IMF, creditor governments, and Mexico, and subnational actors in both the U.S. and Mexico. As has been shown, in the U.S. the Federal Reserve, the Treasury, Defense, and Agriculture Departments, and the OMB were all involved in the negotiations during the first Mexican weekend; each perceived the issue differently and had divergent priorities. The same was true in Mexico, and in that case Silva had to work with a range of decision makers, including some who favored a default announcement and others who were prepared to sign virtually any IMF plan.

Clearly there was no hierarchy of issues which would conform to a realist model of politics during the four months spent crafting the relief plan. Debt relief was the major issue facing Mexico then, and afterwards. The most important security issue facing Mexico and its creditors was financial security. And finally, for obvious reasons there was no role for force during the episode. There was little that any actor could gain by threatening violence; the "financial web" (Astiz, 1983:49-50) in which the actors were caught precluded anyone from utilizing violent means. The processes by which Mexico's debt was managed also reflect complex interdependence. As has already been demonstrated, different actors had divergent goals. Issue linkage beyond international debt was not even tried. For example, the U.S. did not even bother attempting to trade assistance on debt for changes in Mexico's foreign policy; both Presidents Lopez Portillo and de la Madrid pursued Central American peace initiatives to which the U.S. objected (Bagley, 1983:407-408).

Also as the complex interdependence model would suggest, the role of international organizations increased during the Mexican situation. The BIS and the IMF served as forums for discussion of the problem and as actors searching for solutions. They became integral parts of the rescue network which developed. And as the influence of these organizations suggested, power in debt management was not a factor of an actor's ability to mobilize force, but instead of the access to fluid capital which could be moved rapidly, the possession of detailed technical knowledge on negotiating methods, and the capacity to explore policy options and build coalitions while under pressure.

Endnotes

[1]See Table 14 for the exact amounts rescheduled.

[2]On the implications of short term loans, see the discussion in Chapter Five.

[3]In summarizing the discussions this section utilizes, in addition to numerous newpaper accounts, the time line developed by Joseph Kraft in The Mexican Rescue (New York: Group of Thirty, 1984), which is the single most complete account of the subject.

[4]The G-10 in the BIS consists of Belgium, Britain, Canada, France, Italy, Japan, the Netherlands, Sweden, West Germany, and the U.S.

[5]The group, according to Kraft (1984a:22-23) included Chase Manhattan, Chemical, Morgan Guarantee, Bank of America, Bankers Trust, Manufacturers Hanover, Bank of Tokyo, Lloyds, Sociètè Gènèrale of Belgium, Bank of Montreal, Swiss Bank Corporation, Deutsche Bank, and Banomex of Mexico.

CHAPTER EIGHT

BACKING THE IMF:

THE ADMINISTRATION CHANGES DIRECTION

The third "puzzle" in Reagan Administration decision making which has been identified in this study is the official shift in policy toward the International Monetary Fund which occurred in 1982. During its first year the Reagan team had little use for the IMF, but by the end of 1982 it had embraced the organization as an important ally in preventing debt defaults. The Administration's shift was so pronounced it took on the difficult task of seeking over $8 billion of new U.S. funds for the IMF, against robust bipartisan congressional and public opposition. The difficulty the Administration experienced in getting the bill passed, and the compromises it was forced to make to do so, emphasize the magnitude of the policy shift involved.

In the context of the events of the previous two years, the Administration's transformation is easier to understand. With the Polish and Mexican default scares, some of the basic foundations of Reagan economic thinking were obviously shaken. Therefore, while this topic is a discreet, little-noticed and rarely-investigated one in the context of larger Administration policy it should not be ignored. The shift in Reagan policy provides further evidence that the international political economy and the global debt structure differed from the Administration's conceptions, and dictated unexpected policies. It is also another indication of the inadequacy of realist models for explaining the politics of international debt.

Reagan Policy and the IMF

In Chapter Two Administration policy toward international organizations was discussed. It was noted that Reagan officials were skeptical of the utility of such agencies, and that this was reflected in their philosophy and actions.

According to the Administration, many (if not most) international organizations were controlled by small states whose voting power was greater than their actual global or regional influence. Many of these states were headed by leaders with little appreciation for the "magic of the marketplace" which encouraged the production and distribution of goods and services. Because these agencies and their member nation-states had little of their own capital at risk, it was easy for them to lean toward socialist methods of production, and to support anti-capitalist initiatives. Such organizations spent money unwisely and inefficiently, on programs that provided short-term relief but few opportunities for genuine long-range growth.

Agencies like the World Bank and its "soft loan window" the International Development Agency (IDA) were the worst offenders against orthodox free-market wisdom. Budget Director David Stockman and Undersecretary of the Treasury for Monetary Affairs Beryl Sprinkel were the Administration's "point men" in making these arguments; for them the IMF was only marginally palatable (Rowen, 1985b:355).

For support, the Administration could argue it was acting in line with broadly held sentiment in the U.S. For example, Congress had been reluctant to fund fully Carter Administration budget requests for international organizations. It was especially reticent about appropriating public funds for such actors while the Reagan Administration was sharply reducing the pace of domestic social spending. And the American public was equally opposed to increased spending for external agencies; the lack of any strong domestic constituency in favor of higher multilateral spending made it rather easy for the Reagan Administration to deny requests for such funds. Administration rhetoric was largely mirrored by action. One telling example was the composition of foreign aid in the first Reagan term. Because of its skeptical approach toward international agencies, and its conviction that bilateral spending was more likely to foster improved U.S. relations with strategically-placed states, U.S. multilateral aid declined by more than one-half during the first four Reagan budgets. (See Table 15). Another notable example is the way the Reagan Administration dealt with IDA appropriations. The Carter Administration had negotiated a $3.24 billion American pledge for the sixth replenishment of the IDA (known as IDA-6), to be funded from 1981 to 1983 (Farnsworth, 1981b). Because of Reagan objections and congressional obstacles, by mid-1983 the U.S. was over $1 billion behind in funding its pledge, and other states began to reduce their appropriations to match American reticence. Not even the impact of global debt scares could motivate the Administration to support fulfilling the full U.S. commitment (see, for example, Farnsworth, 1981b; Hailey, 1981; Rowen, 1981a; Martin, 1982; Rowen, 1983a, 1983b).

The IMF As Villain

An effective way of demonstrating the Administration's shift regarding the IMF is to investigate how its approach to the organization differed from 1981 to 1982. The best place to start is at the joint annual meeting of the IMF and the World Bank.

TABLE 15

COMPOSITION OF U.S. FOREIGN AID, 1964-1987
(Millions U.S. dollars)

Year	Multilateral Aid	Bilateral Aid	Total	Multilateral as Percent of Total
1964	200	3,240	3,440	6.2
1965	160	3,460	3,620	4.4
1966	110	3,550	3,660	3.0
1967	310	3,410	3,720	8.3
1968	250	3,050	3,300	7.6
1969	330	2,830	3,160	10.4
1970	390	2,660	3,050	12.8
1971	430	2,890	3,320	13.0
1972	630	2,720	3,350	18.9
1973	630	2,340	2,970	21.2
1974	880	2,560	3,440	25.6
1975	1,070	2,940	4,160	30.3
1976	1,050	2,840	3,890	27.0
1977	1,260	2,900	4,160	30.3
1978	2,190	3,470	5,660	38.7
1979	619	4,080	4,690	13.0
1980	2,770	4,370	7,140	38.3
1981	1,470	4,320	5,790	25.4
1982	3,340	4,860	8,200	40.1
1983	2,520	5,560	8,080	30.1
1984	2,250	6,460	8,710	25.8
1985	1,220	8,180	9,400	13.0
1986	1,427	12,443	13,915	10.5
1987	1,187	13,341	12,528	9.4

Source: Development Cooperation (Paris: Organization for Economic Cooperation and Development, 1964-1986), various issues. Cited in Vernon and Spar, 1989:161.

In the Fall 1981 meeting of these agencies, the Reagan Administration, barely in office eight months, sought to 'take its policies global' ("Reagan Takes", 1981). In a speech to the assembled representatives, President Reagan suggested the most important contribution developed states could make to LDCs was to establish "sound economic policies at home". This included reducing the role of government in the economy and demonstrating faith in free market tenets. As exemplified by the U.S., Reagan said, this meant reduced government spending and taxes, and restrained growth in the money supply to allow economic expansion without inflation. Moreover, in answer to those who wanted greater external American financial assistance, Reagan said that constraints in the U.S. economy prevented any increase in spending for external agencies such as the IMF (Farnsworth, 1981a; Silk, 1981).

According to the President, Treasury Secretary Regan, and other U.S. officials in attendance, the IMF needed to adopt similar policies. The Administration made it clear it intended to reverse the Carter finding of the previous year that the effects of the second oil price shock, and related LDC credit problems, necessitated an expansion of IMF capital. On the contrary, said U.S. officials, what the global economy needed was not an increase, but a contraction in liquidity, to reduce international inflationary pressure ("Reagan Set", 1981). U.S. representatives argued that MDBs in general should tighten terms for loans to LDCs, especially to NICs such as Brazil and Mexico; these states should be "graduated" as soon as possible from loans at concessional rates to funding on the open market at regular interest rates (Rowen, 1981b:A6). The overriding problem for most developing states, the Administration maintained, was not a lack of funds but their failure to adjust their economies to external realities. To help foster these goals, the Administration line went, the IMF should be limited to balance-of-payments financing--its original purpose--and not involve itself in Third World development. This implied the IMF's role as a "lender of last resort" should be reestablished; by helping developed states to adjust to payments difficulties the agency could best serve the growth of LDCs.

Lessons and Signals

As previous chapters have demonstrated, a variety of events took place in 1981 and 1982 which caused some in the Administration to rethink the applicability of Reagan policies. These events influenced official assumptions about the self-regulating nature of the international capitalist system, and about the chances international finances would not be manipulated for domestic political purposes. The affairs of these two years suggested the Administration goal of returning the international economy to the characteristics of a past age might have to be delayed.

Globally, by late 1982 debt problems were severe, and the prospects for a "quick fix" were gone. The Polish debt situation had indicated to the Administration that the U.S. could not stand aloof from international debt; with the risks in existence the U.S. was involved whether it wanted to be or not. The mounting Argentine debt (see Table 16), which had nearly become a political pawn after the Falklands war, remained a potential danger area. The Mexican rescue had made the amounts at stake in Poland and Argentina small change by comparison. Brazil threatened to become the next financial hot spot, and it neared default in November 1982. The U.S. produced $1.5 billion in loans to

TABLE 16

SELECTED ECONOMIC INDICATORS, ABM DEBTOR COUNTRIES 1973-1983
(Billion dollars and percentages)

	1973	1974	1975	1976	1977	1978	1979	1980	1981	1982	1983
Argentina											
Total Debt	6.4	8.0	7.9	8.3	9.7	12.5	19.0	27.2	35.7	38.0	44.0
Short-term debt	1.5	2.4	2.6	2.1	2.8	2.6	6.0	9.3	10.0	11.0	NA
Net debt/exports	140.8	145.2	211.5	145.7	96.8	96.1	97.3	182.5	275.3	353.5	486.0
Inflation	62.5	23.1	187.5	447.8	176.6	175.3	159.6	100.8	104.5	164.8	343.8
Brazil											
Total Debt	13.8	18.9	23.3	28.6	35.2	48.4	57.4	66.1	75.7	82.2	91.9
Short-term debt	2.2	4.5	4.3	4.4	4.3	4.9	7.5	12.2	14.3	16.8	NA
Net debt/exports	106.1	145.9	194.3	195.8	207.6	252.2	269.3	259.1	256.6	365.3	336.6
Inflation	13.2	27.3	29.6	41.7	43.3	38.3	52.8	82.8	105.6	98.0	142.0
Mexico											
Total Debt	8.6	12.8	16.9	21.8	27.1	33.6	40.8	53.8	74.1	84.1	87.6
Short-term debt	2.1	3.3	3.6	3.3	3.2	4.6	7.6	15.5	24.0	25.2	NA
Net debt/exports	154.6	182.0	243.8	286.5	309.7	278.2	241.7	205.7	242.4	272.7	308.0
Inflation	12.1	23.5	15.4	15.7	29.0	17.5	18.1	26.4	27.9	59.0	101.9

Source: See Table 14, also Central Bank of Brazil. Cited in Cline, 1984: 258-259, 262-263, 270-271.

Note: Net debt as percentage of exports of goods and services. Consumer price inflation, year over year.

Brasilia in November and December, 1982, and took an active role in developing a $5 billion IMF bridge loan (Purcell, 1983a:669-670).

Regionally, the chances of a political explosion or an economic collapse in the U.S.'s back yard stimulated concern. By mid-1982, after Washington had supported Britain during the Falklands war, the U.S. attempt to discuss collective security arrangements with Latin American nations was a dead issue (Purcell, 1983a:667). The possibility of a response via a coordinated Latin American debt payments moratorium seemed quite real.

Economically, the recession in the U.S. and elsewhere was squeezing Latin American exports, which the Administration had expected would allow the region to "grow its way" out of its debt difficulties. High interest rates continued to siphon wealth away from Latin American countries (Purcell, 1983b:592). The debt and export situation, grim for LDCs generally, was especially bad for ABM states, and getting worse (see Table 16). Even if the Administration had faith in the basic resiliency of the international economy, the exposure of U.S. banks-- which the federal government could only partially protect--posed an immediate danger.

It is in this context that the IMF played its major role in creating the relief package for Mexico. The Administration did not possess more than a few billion dollars which it could move on short notice. By acting quickly, the IMF had gained the confidence of bankers, which helped obtain the delays in payment deadlines. After that, the IMF, under Director de Larosiére, forced the banks to participate in additional lending. For the Reagan Administration, which needed a way to spread and share the burden of dealing with the debt situation, strengthening the IMF seemed to be the most palatable--or least repulsive--option. The result was that by the fall of 1982, less than a year after the Administration had wanted little to do with the Fund, it was willing to discuss a capital increase for the agency (Purcell, 1983b:593).

The IMF As Hero

The Reagan Administration's public "IMF-bashing" came to an end in early September 1982, against the backdrop of the agency's negotiations for an assistance package with Mexico. At a meeting of G-10[1] finance ministers in Toronto just prior to the annual IMF/World Bank meeting, Treasury Secretary Regan announced the U.S. favored a general capital increase (GCI) for the IMF (Farnsworth, 1982a). It had become apparent to many observers in recent months that too much of the IMF's present quota of $67 billion had been loaned or set aside. Another emergency like the Mexican one could leave the organization unable to act, with unknown implications for developed states and LDCs alike ("Change", 1982).

To settle on the exact size of the increase, the IMF's Interim Committee began periodic discussions after the Toronto meeting. It was decided that the organization's 143 member states would be assessed a percentage increase above their present quotas. The negotiations about the amount of GCI were hardly pro forma; too large an amount could prevent crucial states from participating, and a vocal group of states remained concerned about the inflationary potential of a substantial rise in liquidity. A too-small amount could suggest to debtor countries the IMF's members were not serious about their debt and development problems. In Toronto a rise of 25% was discussed, with the sea change created by the U.S. support causing some to advocate an even greater increase (Rowen, 1982).

In retrospect, the reasons for the Administration's shift in position were rather obvious; most of them were used by Reagan officials in lobbying Congress to approve and fund the U.S.'s additional share. One very salient factor was the fact that the U.S. government was accustomed to working with the IMF. The U.S. had been an active member of the organization since its inception nearly four decades earlier; it and its allies had been the heaviest users of the IMF and had benefitted the most from it. Most of the major monetary regime changes of the previous forty years had taken place with some IMF influence. Therefore, of the various multilateral organizations of its type, the IMF was one that seemed rather supportive of international capitalism, especially in comparison to the World Bank and various U.N agencies. The increasingly strict conditionality the IMF had begun to impose upon loan recipients by mid-1982 made it more attractive to the Reagan Administration (Cohen, 1985:150). In fact, had some other international agency sought to increase its financial power as did the IMF in late 1982, the chances of U.S. participation would have been considerably reduced. Aside from the obvious advantage--that the IMF was already there--the Administration believed the increase opened new avenues for U.S. influence (Cohen, 1985:150-151). With the U.S. heavily involved in agency decision making, the IMF could provide Washington with indirect influence; the organization could serve as a buffer between developed states and LDCs. Therefore, the IMF's messages would seem less threatening and nationally motivated, and more impartial. And not only could it influence governments, but the IMF was proving it could pressure banks. With the largest share of votes, the U.S. would have the loudest voice vis-a-vis banks, many of which appeared ready to pull out of LDC lending if they could. In short, "through its ability to shape attitudes at the Fund... Washington could hope to exercise more leverage over debtors and banks indirectly than seemed feasible directly, and at a lower political cost" (Cohen, 1985:150).

Other less far-reaching but nonetheless cogent arguments helped convince the Administration to support the GCI. First, the U.S. would not actually have to provide funds which it would never see again; the money in question would be "deposited", earn interest, and gain the U.S. a claim on a similar value in SDRs ("IMF Funds", 1983:241). Second, a variety of banks supported the increase; their leadership knew the IMF could provide <u>indirect</u> assistance to them, even if they were required to participate in new lending (Bennett, 1982c). Finally, participation would maintain Washington's share of the IMF vote at just under 20%, giving it an effective veto power on most agency decisions. The damage to the American leadership role was inestimable, but potentially large, if the U.S. did not maintain its claim on such power.

Of course, a number of countervailing arguments existed, and would have to be addressed before Congress would approve any money. Perhaps the greatest obstacle was a factor of previous Reagan policy. The Administration's critical, even loathsome approach to the IMF earlier had left the organization with few vocal allies in the White House and among Republicans in Congress. It would prove to be difficult to find a core group of supporters willing to push the measure for legislative approval. As with most foreign aid, the IMF GCI had no natural constituency in Congress or among the public, and the Administration faced an uphill battle with no guarantee of success.

Two other criticisms were raised about the idea. First, it was true that U.S. funds would earn interest while deposited with the IMF, but the deposit would have to be raised in private credit markets. This meant that the federal government would incur interest charges on funds not used directly for the American public, and the effort to borrow the money would place upward pressure on U.S. interest rates. Second, the measure appeared to some a bank bailout. Critics argued that IMF funds would simply be recycled by debtor nations to pay bank loans; the funds would not be used for growth-oriented projects, but to reimburse unwise and greedy bankers. With the Administration reducing domestic spending for social programs, such an increase was certain to face vociferous opposition at home.

Even with the possible obstacles, in the end the Administration decided to support a substantial rise in the IMF's lendable funds. In late November the IMF governors decided on approximately a 50% increase in member quotas (Lewis, 1982b:D1; Pine, 1983c). In early February 1983 final agreement was reached on a \$32.5 billion rise in the organization's lending pool, from \$66 billion to \$98.5 billion[2]. This was a 47.4% increase, far larger than most observers could have foreseen six months earlier. The U.S. share of the increase was set at \$8.4 billion, \$5.8 billion of which was part of the regular fund, and \$2.6 billion for the General Arrangements to Borrow (GAB), a contingency fund for special emergencies (Farnsworth, 1983a).

Strange and Unhappy Bedfellows: The Battle in Congress

As events would have it, getting the Administration to change policy toward the IMF was only slightly more difficult than getting legislative approval for the funding increase. Final congressional action on the measure was not completed until the last day of the Fall 1983 session. The story of the appropriation process would not be germane to this chapter, except that the difficulty the Administration experienced in obtaining the funds indicates how strongly it supported the IMF in 1983.

It is worth noting the Administration sent cabinet and sub-cabinet level officials to appear scores of times before congressional committees and subcommittees, in hopes of gathering votes. Opposition to the measure was bipartisan; liberals viewed it as a bank bailout, while conservatives--following the early Reagan lead--argued it would increase funds being sent to socialist Third World dictatorships. Legislators from both parties attempted to load the measure with "killer amendments" during both committee and floor action. Additional opposition came from public interest groups. Making passage especially challenging was the fact the Administration never received the support of a majority of Republicans on any vote during the process. There was a three month delay in the fall while Democratic leaders held up the bill; Republican congressional officials had sent campaign literature into the districts of Democratic advocates of the bill, accusing them of supporting U.S. funds for communist governments. Not until the Administration sent public expressions of gratitude to the Democrats involved was the legislation allowed to proceed. To finally get the bill approved and the funds appropriated, the Administration had to accept a $15.6 billion housing measure which was attached to the IMF package; Democratic leaders in the House made it clear the IMF bill was dead without the quid pro quo[3].

Conclusions

In helping to increase the role of the IMF in development politics, the Administration bolstered its own cause as well. But the IMF's role as a predominant player in international debt would not last long. Within a few months LDCs began to see the U.S. hand in the IMF's dealings, and grew increasingly resentful (Cohen, 1985:151). The Reagan Administration had won a difficult battle, but the returns were not as great or as durable as it might have hoped. Remaking official U.S. debt policy had proven to be both difficult and expensive.

In explaining the third puzzle of this study, as is often the case attention to the context of the Reagan policy shift reveals an explanation. The Administration choices were limited in late 1982; it was manifest that unilateral policies showed little promise. The Mexican debt scare served to convince Administration personnel that the multilateral approach to debt management was not just less expensive politically and financially, but was necessary because the U.S. no longer had the resources to keep the international financial system stable by itself. Moving into the game now were actors--the banks and the IMF--that the U.S. government could hardly rule and rarely regulate.

The Polish and Mexican debt "crises" brought into the open for many in the Administration the interdependent nature of international debt. Reagan policy from now on would reflect an incipient recognition that the international political and financial systems had changed, and wishing could not deny that.

Endnotes

[1]Belgium, Britain, Canada, France, Italy, Japan, the Netherlands, Sweden, the U.S., and West Germany.

[2]The exact dollar figure mentioned varies among different sources, depending upon when an estimate of the increase is made. This reflects the fact that the size of the rise is measured in special drawing rights, and then converted to dollars, based on a shifting exchange rate. In any case, the exact amount for which the Reagan Administration applied to Congress remained the same.

[3]The information in this paragraph is taken from numerous newspaper and journal articles from the first eleven months of 1983. A brief but adequate account of the struggle in Congress can be found in Michael Glennon, Diane Granat, and Robert Rothman, "IMF-Housing Bargain Cleared By End-of-Session Packaging", Congressional Quarterly Weekly Report 41 (November 19,1983):2457-2458; and "IMF Funds Increased, Ex-Im Bank Extended", Congressional Quarterly Almanac 39 [First Session, 1983] (Washington, D.C.: Congressional Quarterly, Inc.):241-248.

CHAPTER NINE

THE BAKER PLAN: RECOGNIZING INTERDEPENDENCE IN

INTERNATIONAL DEBT

The final puzzle to be addressed in this study involves the "Baker Plan", the Reagan Administration's October 1985 initiative designed to include banks, MDBs--and thereby creditor states--and debtor nations in a program to increase LDC financing. In announcing this plan, the Administration expressed its belief that unilateral, laissez-faire approaches to international debt had not corrected the basic financial problems experienced by developing states.

As with the first three puzzles of Administration policy making, when the Baker Plan is reviewed in the context of the events of the previous three years, the initiative is less surprising. While the period from late 1982 until late 1985 was devoid of major "crises" of the depth and breadth of the Mexican default scare, there remained plenty of reasons for the Administration to be concerned with the international debt situation. These included the generally depressed economic conditions in LDCs (especially in Latin America), discussions among debtor governments of possible debt payments moratoriums, and slow growth in certain sectors of the U.S. economy. By the middle of 1985 the short-lived rebirth of LDC economies was over, and it was impossible for informed U.S. policy makers to argue developed states would inevitably accept the present structure of the global financial system.

It was in this context that two dramatic shifts in U.S. foreign economic policy took place. The first, and indirectly relevant to the present discussion, was the September 1985 agreement by the Administration on the need for international manipulation of exchange rates. The second shift involved the announcement of the Baker Plan. These two events signified that broad systemic constraints had helped force a dramatic change in the way the Administration conducted business. Now the Reagan team embraced multilateralism--perhaps not as strongly as it had adopted unilateral policies before 1985, but convincingly enough to indicate that even "realist" policy makers saw some value in alternative approaches to the international system.

Hard Lessons, Difficult Choices

The events of the three years after the Mexican bailout presented a mixed image of the global economy. Both optimism and pessimism over the future of developed states' and LDCs' economies could be justified, depending on which data one emphasized.

The Global Outlook

During 1983 and 1984 observers could find certain positive signs about LDC economic performance. As Table 17 indicates, a broad study of LDCs showed that their ratio of debt to exports declined from 1983 to 1984, and debt service in both years was lower than in 1982. The percentage of privately held debt dropped from 1983 to 1984, leading some to see less danger of defaults caused by inflexible bankers. As Table 18 indicates, the amount transferred to major debtors from official creditors rose significantly from 1983 to 1984, both overall and to Latin America. The IMF estimated capital importers reduced their cumulative current account deficit from $112.5 billion in 1981 to $37.9 billion in 1984, despite having to borrow at higher interest rates (Bogdanowicz-Bindert, 1985-1986:265).

There were also encouraging signs in Latin America, the region of greatest financial interest to the U.S. In mid-1983 Brazil received large-scale assistance from the U.S. in the form of $1.5 billion in loan guarantees from the Export-Import Bank (Cohen, 1985:145), and the Fed continued to push U.S. banks to restore deposits it had removed from Brazilian banks ("Volcker", 1983). In September 1983 the IMF arranged $11 billion in credits and loans to Brasilia for the remainder of 1983 and all of 1984, in a deal involving creditor governments and commercial and development banks (Farnsworth, 1983h:A1). The mood of international investors and bankers brightened further in late 1984, when Mexico and its creditors worked out a multiyear formula for rescheduling its debt; the arrangement entailed spreading Mexico's obligations over the following fourteen years (Hartland-Thunberg, 1986:14). Coupled with these trends was the general improvement in the U.S. and OECD economies, including a rise in American imports of Latin American products (Hartland-Thunberg, 1986:16; Sachs, 1986:401). These events allowed the Reagan Administration to lower international debt on the political agenda.

But a closer look at economic trends revealed certain LDC problems had not been effected by the expansion in developed states' economies. Some trends were masked by otherwise good news in 1983 and 1984; some only became apparent in 1985. They revealed a handful of the heaviest debtors struggling to remain solvent.

TABLE 17

DEBT INDICATORS FOR ALL DEVELOPING COUNTRIES IN SELECTED YEARS, 1970-1985
(Percent)

	1970	1874	1976	1978	1980	1981	1982	1983	1984	1985
Ratio of debt to GNP	14.1	15.4	18.1	21.0	21.1	22.8	26.8	31.8	32.7	33.0
Ratio of debt to exports	108.9	80.0	100.2	113.1	90.1	97.5	116.4	134.3	130.4	135.7
Debt-service ratio	14.7	11.8	13.6	18.4	16.1	17.7	20.7	19.4	19.8	21.9
Ratio of interest service to GNP	0.5	0.8	0.8	1.1	1.6	1.9	2.4	2.4	2.6	2.7
Total debt outstanding and disbursed (billions)	$68	$141	$204	$313	$432	$493	$552	$630	$674	$711
Private sources of debt as percentage of total	50.9	56.5	59.0	61.5	63.3	64.5	64.9	66.1	65.7	64.5

Source: World Bank, World Development Report 1985, p. 24, Table 2.6; and World Development Report 1986, p. 32, Table 2.11. Cited in Committee for Economic Development, 1988:121.

Note: Data based on sample of ninety developing countries.

TABLE 18

NET RESOURCE TRANSFERS TO DEBTOR COUNTRIES, 1981-1984
(Billions of Dollars)

Category	1981	1982	1983	1984
Major debtor countries				
Official creditors	5.7	5.4	1.5	4.6
Private creditors	4.8	1.0	-1.8	-10.0
Latin America				
Official creditors	2.6	3.0	1.8	3.2
Private creditors	4.0	0.4	-3.5	-10.9
Sub-Saharan Africa				
Official creditors	3.3	3.2	3.3	2.0
Private creditors	1.7	2.6	1.8	-2.1

Source: World Bank, World Debt Tables: External Debt of Developing Countries, 1985-1986. Cited in Sachs, 1986:407.

TABLE 19

SOURCES OF CAPITAL FLOWS FOR 15 MOST HEAVILY
INDEBTED NATIONS, 1980-1985
(Billions of Dollars)

	1980	1981	1982	1983	1984	1985
Private Creditors	40.7	55.73	2.7	-2.8	4.5	-3.8
Official Creditors (long-term borrowing)	4.6	6.5	4.0	12.0	8.1	4.9
Reserve-related liabilities	1.7	1.6	12.9	14.2	3.2	-2.0
	47.0	63.8	49.6	23.4	15.8	-0.9

Source: IMF, World Economic Outlook, April 1986, Table A42. Cited in Challenge, September/October 1986, p. 55.

Note: Reserve-related liabilites include IMF credit, arrears, and short-term government to government financing.

TABLE 20

SELECTED ECONOMIC INDICATORS IN HEAVILY INDEBTED COUNTRIES 1969-1985

	Average 1969-1978	1979	1980	1981	1982	1983	1984	1985
Per capita GDP (annual change)	3.6	3.6	2.6	-1.6	-2.7	-5.5	-0.1	0.9
Inflation (annual rate)	28.5	40.8	47.4	53.2	57.7	90.8	116.4	126.9
Gross capital formation (percent of GDP)	NA	24.9	24.7	24.5	22.3	18.2	17.4	16.5
Debt-export ratio	NA	182.3	167.1	201.4	269.8	289.7	272.1	284.2

Source: IMF, World Economic Outlook, April 1987. Cited in Sachs, ed., 1989:2.

Note: Data refer to fifteen heavily indebted countries: Argentina, Bolivia, Brazil, Chile, Colombia, Ivory Coast, Ecuador, Mexico, Morocco, Nigeria, Peru, Philippines, Uruguay, Venezuela, Yugoslavia. Inflation refers to consumer price index.

TABLE 21

DEBT-GNP OR GDP RATIO, TOP TWENTY COUNTRIES, 1983 AND 1985

	1983	1985
Zaire	1.54	--
Ivory Coast	1.17	1.62
Israel	1.16	1.18
Ireland	1.13	--
Costa Rica	1.09	1.10
Jamaica	1.00	1.91
Portugal	0.95	0.71
Morocco	0.92	--
Chile	0.89	1.26
Uruguay	0.82	0.89
Peru	0.80	0.81
Panama	0.78	--
Philippines	0.77	0.80
Sudan	0.73	--
Honduras	0.72	0.92
Iceland	0.71	--
Argentina	0.71	0.73
Jordan	0.66	1.06
Mexico	0.61	0.55
Bolivia	0.60	1.33

Source: "World Debt in Crisis: Per Capita Picture," Wall Street Journal, June 22, 1984; World Bank, World Development Report 1987, Tables 3 and 16. Cited in Darity and Horn, 1988:181.

Note: Where information is missing, insufficient data existed for a debt-GNP ratio to be determined. The authors indicate, however, "it is probably safe to say the debt-GNP ratio worsened for all of them. The ratios of public long-term debt alone to GDP were estimated to be 1.00 for Zaire, 0.95 for Morocco, 0.67 for Panama, and 0.73 for the Sudan in 1985."

As Table 17 indicates, for some ninety LDCs, the ratio of debt to GNP rose dramatically from 1982 to 1985, as did the debt to export ratio between 1984 and 1985. The same was true for their debt service ratio. And the down side to the reduction in private lending was its indication that commercial banks desired to abandon LDC funding faster than official creditors could respond. The trend was especially pronounced in Latin America and Sub-Saharan Africa from 1981 to 1984 (see Table 18).

TABLE 22

SELECTED ECONOMIC INDICATORS, MAJOR LDC DEBTORS, 1985

	Total External Debt (billions of dollars)	Debt Service as Percentage of Exports of Goods and Services	Debt-Export Ratio (Total External Debt/1985 Exports)
Brazil	106.7	34.8	4.17
Mexico	97.4	48.2	4.45
Argentina	48.4	--	5.76
South Korea	48.0	21.5	1.58
Indonesia	35.8	25.1	1.92
Venezuela	32.1	--	2.61
Poland	27.0	--	--
Philippines	26.2	19.5	5.57
Turkey	26.1	32.1	3.14
Chile	20.2	44.1	5.46
Yugoslavia	19.4	21.2	1.71
Nigeria	18.3	32.1	1.09
Peru	13.7	16.0	--
Ivory Coast	8.4	--	2.80

Source: World Bank, World Development Report 1987, Tables 10, 16, 18. Source for Poland in 1983 is "A Wall Street Journal Watch List," Wall Street Journal, June 22, 1984. Cited in Darity and Horn, 1988:179, 183, 185.

The figures were particularly bleak for the fifteen most heavily indebted countries, forced to absorb sizable outflows of funds to banks which were only partially offset by official sources (see Table 19). The problem was compounded by IMF regulations which prevented additional lending to nation-states not in compliance with austerity plans (Farnsworth, 1985b:13), and an inability of the Administration and the Federal Reserve to force much new bank lending ("Third World Debt", 1984). Further afflicting these heaviest debtors was accelerating inflation (despite depressed growth rates) and worsening debt to export figures (see Table 20). The trends were reflected in declining debt to GNP ratios (see Table 21).

The most important result of these trends was a net resource transfer out of LDCs at the worst possible time, when these states needed to compete with developed countries for investment funds. As the data in Tables 19-23 indicate, the situation from 1983 to 1985 was the reverse of the condition found during the expansion of LDC debt during the first part of the decade. By 1985, reduced economic performance and investment in debtor countries merely encouraged more of the same, as

TABLE 23

LATIN AMERICAN DEBT-EXPORT RATIOS, 1981-1985
(percent)

	1981	1982	1983	1984	1985
Argentina	333.4	447.3	458.6	489.7	509.0
Brazil	277.5	356.8	376.7	330.8	348.6
Chile	276.8	332.8	361.2	399.7	414.5
Colombia	150.1	183.0	243.1	248.2	245.9
Ecuador	198.2	232.7	259.5	243.4	254.1
Mexico	243.3	304.1	323.6	291.5	326.9
Peru	229.4	270.9	323.8	335.0	368.1
Venezuela	118.4	154.5	197.9	171.7	181.2

Source: Data Resources, Inc., Latin American Review (Lexington [MA]: DRI, Summer 1986). Cited in Sachs, 1986:411.

the rush by banks to lend them money in earlier years had exacerbated the debt "crisis".

Trouble In the Backyard

Clearly, problems existed for LDCs in general. But especially severe were the difficulties found by mid-1985 in Latin America. For the Reagan Administration the situation was worsened by the fact that by then any goodwill engendered toward the U.S. by its assistance to Mexico had largely disappeared (Cohen, 1985:142). New initiatives by Washington were needed to restore any role for the U.S. as a leader in dealing with the debt problem.

One conclusion easily reached by the Administration was that it could not expect Latin American nations to remain "patient" indefinitely. For these states, the 1980s were becoming the "lost decade" in terms of economic growth. Despite supposedly expanding export markets in developed states, debt to export ratios were worsening dramatically (see Table 23). After a brief improvement the year before, in 1985 terms of trade and export volume again declined (see Table 24). Protectionism in developed states did not help matters (Riding, 1985:D6), and neither did population growth and capital flight (Loomis, 1985). In fact, during the first half of the decade only one state in the region--Panama--reported positive growth in its cumulative per capita GDP (see Table 25). New bank lending to Latin America was virtually nonexistent (see Bouchet, 1987:122). As Table 26 indicates, through interest payments and repatriated foreign profits the region was actually losing tens of billions of dollars annually, and at an accelerating pace (see also Sachs, 1986:406).

TABLE 24

ECONOMIC INDICATORS OF DEBTOR COUNTRIES, 1981-1985
(Annual percent change unless indicated)

Indicator	1981	1982	1983	1984	1985
Countries with debt-servicing problems					
Per capita real GDP	-1.0	-2.5	-4.8	0.2	0.6
Trade balance (billion dollars)	-19.4	-6.0	22.0	34.6	35.4
Terms of trade	-2.8	-4.8	-2.8	2.7	-2.5
Export volume	-3.0	-4.2	5.4	7.0	1.4
Debt-export ratio (percent)	180.2	234.5	252.3	244.2	260.2
Western Hemisphere					
Per capita real GDP	-1.2	-3.2	-5.3	0.8	1.7
Trade balance (billion dollars)	-3.2	7.2	28.7	37.0	33.6
Terms of trade	-4.4	-5.8	-2.8	4.0	-3.0
Export volume	6.1	-2.2	7.1	7.3	-2.1
Debt-export ratio (percent)	208.8	267.2	287.5	273.3	295.0
Sub-Saharan Africa					
Per capita real GDP	-1.2	-2.8	-2.8	-1.4	0.9
Trade balance (billion dollars)	-4.5	-3.9	-1.6	0.6	0.1
Terms of trade	-7.3	-6.5	1.2	5.0	-2.0
Export volume	-2.6	4.4	0.4	4.9	0.7
Debt-export ratio (percent)	169.3	201.3	215.8	216.3	240.3

Source: IMF, World Economic Outlook, April 1986. Cited in Sachs: 1986, p. 400.

Perhaps most ominously, the Administration had to be concerned with the possibility of a "debtor's cartel" which would halt debt payments. In January 1984 foreign ministers of Argentina, Brazil, Columbia, Ecuador, Mexico, Peru, and Venezuela, and observers from Bolivia, Chile, the Dominican Republic, and Uruguay, met in Cartegena, Columbia to discuss collective debt strategies (Riding, 1984). In May 1984 the presidents of Latin America's four largest debtor states--Argentina, Brazil, Columbia, and Mexico--met in Buenos Aires. They issued a joint statement which said their countries could not indefinitely endure the costs of externally-mandated adjustment strategies (Cohen, 1985:147). The next month the representatives which had assembled in Columbia in January officially formed the Cartegena Group; they met often during 1984 and 1985 to discuss debt service ceilings and the chances of taking concerted action on interest rates and IMF austerity policies (Pollin and Zepeda, 1988:106-107). Also adding his voice to the topic was Fidel Castro, who spoke often during 1984 and 1985 on the need for an indefinite Latin debt payments moratorium. Most clearly, at his inauguration in July 1985, Peru's new president Alan Garcia Perez said his country would cap interest and principal payments at 10% of its export earnings (Loomis, 1985:102). He reiterated his message in a speech to the UN General Assembly in which he said his nation's choice was either 'debt or democracy' (Bogdanowicz-Bindert, 1985-1986:259).

TABLE 25

CHANGE IN REAL PER CAPITA GDP, LATIN AMERICAN STATES 1981-1985 (percent)

Country	Cumulative Change
Argentina	-18.5
Bolivia	-28.4
Brazil	-2.0
Chile	-8.7
Colombia	-0.1
Costa Rica	-11.2
Ecuador	-3.9
El Salvador	-24.0
Guatemala	-18.3
Jamaica	-2.2
Mexico	-4.3
Panama	0.7
Peru	-14.8
Uruguay	-18.6
Venezuela	-21.6

Source: United Nations Economic Commission for Latin America and the Caribbean, "The Economic Crisis: Policies for Adjustment, Stabilization, and Growth" (Mexico City: April 1986). Cited in Sachs, 1986:410.

Note: Data for Jamaica is to 1984.

TABLE 26

NET RESOURCE TRANSFERS TO LATIN AMERICA, 1981-1985
(Billions of dollars)

Year	Net capital inflow	—	Interest repayments and foreign profits	= =	Net Resource Transfer
1981	49.1		27.8		21.3
1982	27.6		36.8		-9.2
1983	6.1		34.9		-28.8
1984	11.6		37.1		-25.5
1985	4.1		36.7		-32.6

Source: Inter-American Development Bank, Economic and Social Progress in Latin America, 1986 Report (Washington [D.C.]: IDB, 1986), p. 35, Table III-8. Cited in Sachs, 1986:400.

Note: Data for 1985 are preliminary.

The New Team In Washington

Changing events had much to do with the Reagan Administration's shift in debt policy in late 1985. Also included were a number of decision makers who were either not involved in earlier Reagan policy making, or were active to a lesser degree.

The most notable figure was obviously Treasury Secretary James Baker, the former Chief of Staff who had traded positions with Donald Reagan in January 1985. During the first Reagan term Baker absorbed the Administration's rationale behind laissez-faire exchange rate and lending policies (Evans, 1986:91). He also developed an interest in international debt and became convinced austerity was not the best way for developing states to conquer their balance of payments problems. Upon becoming Treasury Secretary he identified several potential threats posed to the American economy by LDC debt, including risks to the banking system, and the effects of lengthy debtor stagnation on U.S. exports and employment (Bogdanowicz-Bindert, 1985-1986:267).

Reports suggest Baker was exceptionally well placed to exert a dramatic change in the way the Administration made foreign economic policy (Kilborn, 1985c). Baker had not been involved in Administration policy toward the IDA and World Bank, and therefore did not need to be concerned about appearing indecisive over closer relationships with the agencies. Baker and Deputy Treasury Secretary Richard Darman began discussing the possibility of a coordinated effort by the IMF and World Bank to deal with Third World debt; one idea involved the IMF rendering short term assistance in redressing liquidity problems, with the World Bank then assisting in creating longer term development plans (Rowen, 1985b:358). Baker and Darman proceeded to develop a network of like-minded individuals from within the Administration, and brought into this network Paul Volcker, who had been seeking ways to entice banks to lend more in developing areas. Secretary of State George Schultz also lent his support; he was concerned about the chances of political upheaval in Latin America. During the spring and summer of 1985, Baker, Darman, Schultz, Volcker, and a number of aides from the State and Treasury departments met every week to ten days for breakfast meetings, and discussed U.S. options (Rowen, 1986:304, 307).

The group became convinced more pragmatic policies toward LDC debt were in order, because of the implications of that debt both external and internal to the U.S. (Bogdanowicz-Bindert, 1985-1986:260). Externally, the decision makers recognized that the extant U.S. debt strategy, which had entailed modest LDC growth coupled with a modicum of private external funding (see Purcell, 1983b:591), had failed. In Latin America, for example, the threat of another crisis like that of 1982 was real, but no savior was guaranteed to appear this time. In the fall of 1985, Mexico, which just the previous year had being hailed as an example of a successfully adjusting debtor state, found itself suffering from declining oil prices and a devastating earthquake, and needed short-term rescheduling on nearly a billion dollars of debt payments (Riding, 1985:D6). In addition, the chances of a debtor cartel taking action were impossible to estimate accurately, but clearly raised concerns.

Within the U.S., Baker and his allies in the Treasury department noted the slowing of growth in the American economy, and recessions in the agriculture and manufacturing sectors. Protectionist sentiment in Congress ran high, even with the possibility of retaliation by other exporting nations. The Administration wanted to avoid any actions that would close off foreign markets to U.S. goods. At the same time it recognized the needs of Mexico and Brazil for export markets in which to gain foreign exchange for debt service (Bogdanowicz-Bindert, 1985-1986:259); both had already felt the impact of developed states' protectionism on their exports (Riding, 1985:D6).

A New Pragmatism?

By the fall of 1985 there were clear signs from the Administration that 'the ideologues had been replaced by pragmatists".[1] The Plaza accords and the Baker Plan both reflected this shift. The Plaza accords are not directly relevant to a discussion about international debt, but the Administration's shift in policy on exchange rates helps to demonstrate the changes in its outlook. Active management of currencies had always been antithetical to Administration doctrine, because of the assumption that capital should flow freely in an open market. As late as July 1985, G-10 finance ministers meeting in Tokyo had determined that the floating rate system was best left alone, even with the high U.S. dollar distorting global import and export patterns.

But two months later the U.S. was ready to accept a change. On Sunday, September 22 at the Plaza Hotel in New York, G-5[2] finance ministers and central bankers met to discuss strategies for joint intervention in the exchange markets. Baker placed the U.S. firmly behind intervention, and he had the support of Schultz, who had been a long-time supporter of floating rates (Rowen, 1986:307,309). The U.S. joined the other states in agreeing the dollar was overvalued, and needed to be forced downward. For all practical purposes this move on the part of the U.S. constituted an admission that the market had failed on the dollar. After four years of relative disinterest in attempts to direct monetary values, the Plaza initiatives strengthened the role and image of the U.S. within the G-5 forum (Kilborn, 1985c). In addition to changing its policies on exchange values, the Reagan Administration, with Baker as Treasury Secretary, had begun looking for a way to ease the LDC debt burden (especially in Latin America) so that debt moratoriums and political unrest could be avoided and these states could be returned to creditworthy status (Loomis, 1985:98). Both Baker and Schultz saw the need for a growth-oriented, multiyear plan. Their goal was to involve all the major actors in international debt; this included substantial roles for both the IMF and World Bank, and commercial banks as well. They also hoped to create a plan that would allow a case-by-case approach to debt relief, as bankers objected to debt assistance that signalled the international financial system itself was to blame for debtor problems (Rowen, 1986:307).

The way the Administration "test-marketed" its plan reflected the need it felt for broad support by various actors. The Administration sent only its most important officials to sell the initiative to the financial community. In Washington on October 1, Baker and Volcker presented the plan to representatives of Citibank, Chase Manhattan, Bank of America, and Chemical Bank (Kilborn, 1985a). In Seoul on October 5, before the annual IMF/World Bank meeting, Baker met in secret with G-5 finance ministers to reveal the particulars of the package and to seek their support (Farnsworth, 1985b:1). Treasury Department officials spent many hours in Seoul talking with their counterparts from other nations about the U.S. proposal. By the time the Treasury Secretary presented the "Program for Sustained Growth" to the assembled delegates on October 8, the Administration believed it had widespread support for a major change in the politics of international debt.

The Baker Plan

The proposal the Reagan Administration announced in Seoul suggested a multilateral debt relief package for fifteen middle income debtor countries (see Table 27). These states were chosen for a variety of

TABLE 27

BAKER PLAN TARGET COUNTRIES

Country	Foreign Debt (Billions)	1985 Interest		Amount Owed U.S. Banks (Billions)
		(Billions)	Est. % 1985 GNP	
Brazil	103.5	11.8	5.8%	23.8
Mexico	97.7	10.0	6.3%	25.8
Argentina	50.8	5.1	7.9%	8.1
Venezuela	32.6	4.1	8.1%	10.6
Philippines	27.4	2.1	6.2%	5.5
Chile	21.9	2.1	12.9%	6.6
Yugoslavia	20.0	1.7	3.6%	2.4
Nigeria	18.0	1.8	1.9%	1.5
Morocco	14.4	1.0	8.2%	0.9
Peru	13.9	1.3	10.8%	2.1
Colombia	13.9	1.3	3.3%	2.6
Ecuador	7.9	0.7	6.0%	2.2
Ivory Coast	6.3	0.6	8.7%	0.5
Uruguay	4.9	0.5	9.8%	1.0
Bolivia	4.2	0.4	10.0%	0.2
Total	$437.4	$44.5	Average 7.3%	$93.8

Source: Fortune, December 23, 1985, p. 101.

reasons. A number of Latin American debtors were included because of the severity of their financial burdens, and the possibility of the creation of a regional debtor cartel. But because the Administration wanted the support of MDBs and commercial banks, it included five nations from other areas of interest to creditors. The fifteen nations were not necessarily the heaviest debtors in relation to GNP, but they were considered strategically important in political or economic terms. Moreover, of the $437.5 billion in external debt held by these states, $275 billion was owed to commercial banks. U.S. banks were owed $94 billion of this; 84% of that amount was owed to the 24 largest American banks (Loomis, 1985:98).

The Baker Plan had "three essential and mutually reinforcing elements" (Baker, 1985:293). Together they reflected the Administration's desire to maintain a commitment to free-market economics, and yet encourage coordination in managing international debt.

First, Baker called for structural change in the principal debtors. Debtor nations, the Treasury Secretary argued, could expect neither additional external lending nor sustained economic development without becoming competitive within the international economy. Accordingly, Baker stated, the U.S. supported "institutional and structural policies" which included (1985:295):

--increased reliance on the private sector, and less reliance on government, to help increase employment, production and efficiency;

--supply-side actions to mobilize domestic savings and facilitate efficient investment, both domestic and foreign, by means of tax reform, labor market reform and development of financial markets; and

--market opening measures to encourage foreign direct investment and capital inflows, as well as to liberalize trade, including the reduction of export subsidies.

But the adoption of such policies, Baker said, did not mean "fiscal, monetary, and exchange rate policies" that had been the focus of previous LDC goals could now be ignored. "Indeed", he claimed, "macroeconomic policies have been central to efforts to date and must be strengthened to achieve greater progress". Such policies included (1985:295-296):

--market oriented exchange rate, interest rate, wage and pricing policies to promote greater economic efficiency and responsiveness to growth and employment opportunities; and

--sound monetary and fiscal policies focused on reducing domestic imbalances and inflation and on freeing resources for the private sector.

Second, Baker stated the U.S. supported the enhanced effectiveness of international financial institutions. The Secretary lauded the role to date of the IMF in encouraging market-oriented reforms in developing states, and suggested it was now appropriate for the Fund to work closely with the World Bank in pursuit of those objectives. In fact, Baker proposed increased involvement in LDC debt management by the World Bank and its regional development banks. This included a more rapid pace to MDB lending than in the past. Specifically, the Inter-American Development Bank (IDB) could increase its lending by 50% over its yearly $6 billion total to Latin American developing states. In a dramatic departure from previous Administration policy, Baker suggested the World Bank "should assist, both in a technical and financial capacity, those countries which wish to 'privatize' their state-owned enterprises, which in too many cases aggravate already serious budget deficit problems". And "given the importance of increasing commercial bank flows to the principal debtors", Baker said, "there is also an urgent need for efforts to expand the Bank's co-financing operations" with those banks. If the need presented itself, and if progress was made toward the development of a cooperative network of commercial banks, MDBs, and market-oriented LDCs, the secretary announced the U.S. "would be prepared to look seriously at the timing and scope of a general capital increase" for the World Bank (1985:298).

Finally, Baker announced the Administration sought increased lending by the international banking community. The Administration, he noted, was very concerned about the decline in private lending to developing states (1985:299):

> If creditor governments, in an age of budget austerity, are to be called upon to support increases in multilateral development bank lending to the debtor nations, and if the recipient nations are asked to adopt sound economic policies for growth to avoid wasting that financing, then there must also be a commitment by the banking community--a commitment to help the global community make the necessary transition to stronger growth.

> Our assessment of the commitment required by the banks to the entire group of heavily indebted, middle income developing countries would be net new lending in the range of $20 billion for the next three years. In addition, it would be necessary that countries now receiving adequate financing from banks on a voluntary basis continue to do so, provided they maintain sound policies.

Baker called for commercial banks to publicly pledge such funding, for both short-term financing and long-term investment needs, if debtor countries "also make similar growth-oriented policy commitments as their part of the cooperative effort" (1985:298).

All told, the Administration had proposed an increase of $29 billion in new lending to developing states over the following three years. Commercial banks were to supply $20 billion, which amounted to an increase of 2.5% per year in new loans; this figure seems small, but was actually sizable in comparison to the near zero percent growth rate at the time (Bogdanowicz-Bindert, 1985-1986:268). The World Bank and its regional development banks were to raise their new lending $3 billion for each of the three years; the possibility was held out that the IMF might also increase its activities. All these possibilities were contingent upon recipient states making market-oriented reforms.

Conclusions

Economically, the Baker Plan was never really a success. Over the following three to five years, bank lending did not increase nearly the amount called for in the initiative (see Chapter 10), and the excitement it engendered among some actors lasted only a short time. Nonetheless, the Baker Plan was the most obvious official concession by the Reagan Administration that the debt problem was serious and long-term, and that austerity in debtor countries was not a substitute for growth (Bogdanowicz-Bindert, 1985-1986:268). It also reflected the Administration's recognition that unilateral policies to deal with the debt "crisis" were likely to fail, although it was not above trying to mold new policies to support its preferences for the international economy. As Baker stated in Seoul (1985:294):

> In today's highly interdependent world economy, efforts at economic isolationism are doomed to failure. Countries which are not prepared to undertake basic adjustments and work within the framework of the case-by-case debt strategy, cooperating with the international financial institutions, cannot expect to benefit from this three-point program. Additional lending will not occur. Efforts by any country to "go it alone" are likely to seriously damage its prospects for future growth.

ENDNOTES

[1]Kilborn (1985c) attributes the observation to Rimmer de Vries, senior international economist at Morgan Guaranty Trust.

[2]Britain, France, Japan, the U.S., and West Germany.

CHAPTER TEN

CONCLUSION: THEORY, FOREIGN POLICY, AND DEBT

This final chapter is divided into three parts. The first offers a summary of the argument made in the previous chapters. The second discusses the possible future for complex interdependence as an analytic tool. The third develops some thoughts about U.S. debt policy through the beginnings of the Bush Administration.

Summary

The main goal of this study has been to explain four "puzzles" of Reagan Administration policy making in international debt. At first glance, given the Administration's stated economic and political goals, and its conception of the international system, the actions it took in each of these cases are contradictory to expectations. As discussed in Chapter One, the cases include:

first, the Administration's decision in early 1982 to pay interest due from Poland to U.S. banks on hundreds of millions of dollars of agricultural credits,

second, the Administration's actions in the late summer and fall of 1982 to prevent a default by Mexico on its international debt,

third, the decision by Reagan officials in late 1982 to support an increase of $8.4 billion in the U.S. share of the lending quota for the International Monetary Fund, and

fourth, the Administration's announcement in October 1985 of a "Plan for Sustained Growth" designed to increase dramatically the amount of money lent to developing countries.

Chapters Two through Nine demonstrate that the "complex interdependence" framework of analysis of the international system developed by Keohane and Nye (1977) more accurately describes the politics of international debt than does the realist model implicitly adopted by the Reagan Administration. Therefore, as stated in Chapter One, a secondary goal in this study has been to stimulate new discussion about the applicability of complex interdependence to international affairs.

Chapters Two through Five develop the theoretical portion of the discussion. Chapter Two, for instance, provides a brief review of the particulars of realism as a school of thought in international relations theory, and profiles the foreign policies nation-states can be expected to pursue in conditions of realism. It then places early Reagan policies firmly within the realist "camp", both in official statements and actions. Chapter Three recognizes the dissatisfaction of some scholars with the theoretical and practical implications of realism. It summarizes the theoretical portion of Keohane and Nye's Power and Interdependence (1977), in which the authors develop the idea of "complex interdependence" to explain much of the dynamics of the international system. Complex interdependence, Keohane and Nye suggest, refers to the rise of mutually dependent relationships among states and non-state actors in certain issue areas. Traditional models of international politics are not always adequate to explain the distribution of capabilities in the contemporary international system, they argue; nor can these methods explain the changing nature of policy making where "power" is no longer primarily a military concept.

Chapter Four concentrates on Keohane and Nye's demonstration of complex interdependence in the oceans space and resources and monetary affairs issue areas. They choose oceans and money as test cases because they have been vital topics since the nineteenth century, and this allows for the testing of their approach to complex interdependence "under changing political and economic conditions" (1977:63). The authors conclude that at various times over the previous five decades complex interdependence has competed with realism to describe more accurately the patterns of politics within these issue areas. Generally, they say, the evidence indicates "that traditional theories of world politics, as applied to oceans and monetary politics, are becoming less useful", and that "with respect to trends in the conditions of world politics over the past half century, the complex interdependence ideal type seems to be becoming increasingly relevant" (1977:161).

Chapter Five should be considered a crucial chapter. It seeks to investigate the politics of external debt in the same way Keohane and Nye study oceans and money. This is done to illustrate the plausibility of a complex interdependence interpretation of international debt. It begins by tracing the rise in international lending in the 1970s and early 1980s, the growth in LDC debt totals by 1981, and the way in which "the music stopped" in 1982 when new lending to developing states nearly ended. It then identifies the "conditions" and "processes" of complex interdependence which Keohane and Nye develop, and explains how they work in international debt.

Most importantly, Chapter Five seeks to complete a task set forth in the first chapter. It was argued there that within international relations there is a widely held understanding of foreign policy as dictated by conditions of realism. But because Keohane and Nye develop complex interdependence at the systemic level, there is no corresponding model of foreign policy for their framework. To demonstrate the Reagan Administration was forced to act under conditions of complex interdependence requires a model against which the policies and actions of states in such situations can be assessed. Therefore, by working from Keohane and Nye's conceptual outline, and with regard to the application of their model to the politics of oceans, money, and debt, the following characteristics of complex interdependence in foreign policy were suggested:

The Structure of Political Power

The role of force. Obviously, the weaker the state the less likely it will be to use force, if it expects stronger actors to respond in kind. More important, however, is the expectation that the greater the degree of mutual dependence among actors--that is, interdependence--the less likely will be the chances actors will apply military means in pursuit of goals. The more issues in which states share such a relationship, the less likely will they each be to damage general ties over narrow differences that do not threaten basic values.

This is not to say that some states may not prefer, or even attempt, to use force. But the more pervasive the mutual dependence, and the greater the depth of its recognition among policy making elites, the less likely is force to be a credible threat. Policy makers may attempt to tie agreements on nonsecurity issues to issues of mutual defense (as in monetary affairs), but this is actually far removed from the realist suggestion that military prowess is a commodity readily applied for settling disagreements.

Absence of a hierarchy of issues. As Keohane and Nye show in monetary politics, military security may rise to the top of the policy agenda in times of external threat. In the final analysis, the territorial integrity of a state is a paramount goal, and one of the reasons for a state's existence. But in situations of complex interdependence, as often as not other issues--either as broad as "economic prosperity" or as narrow as "international debt"--will serve as high politics. Security in the traditional sense does not disappear from concern; rather it is held in abeyance. Decision makers in interdependent states will have in mind their own hierarchies of issues; the more accurately government officials in one state recognize hierarchies held by leaders in other states, the more likely they will be able to pursue mutually beneficial policies. The reverse is also expected, of course.

Multiple channels of contact. In complex interdependence, all actors will have to face a large variety of other actors. With the breaking of the dominance of military security, and the concomitant rise of other issues, new actors will be bound to complicate the policy agenda in almost any issue area. Policy making will become more complex than in realist conditions, and may require more effort by decision makers to design and maintain coherent policies. If actors do not realize the variety of forces involved, their miscalculation will lead to their efforts being frustrated. Moreover, the novelty of these situations may lengthen the time involved in the search for appropriate policies and the means to pursue them.

The Political Process

Actor goals. The higher an issue is on the national policy agenda, the more attention it can be expected to receive from policy elites. The chances of rational, interrelated policy goals being promulgated increase with the amount of attention being given by the decision making elites. All other things remaining equal (admittedly a dangerous assumption), if this happens the chances of policy success increase.

Policy instruments. For the reasons mentioned in the previous section, force will rarely be used. For interdependent states, the requirements for successful policies have changed. Contemporary state leaders will need to recognize these changes, and devote resources to 1) measuring the amount of interdependence which exists in an issue area, and finding ways to affect that, 2) keeping close tabs on transnational actors, and 3) taking an active role in international organizations, if not to dictate policies at least to lead in their development.

Agenda formation. Under more modern conditions, the political agenda will be set by the distribution of power in particular issue areas, and by the ability of regimes to adjust to the demands placed on them by events and actors. It can be expected that former hegemons will experience difficulty in setting the agenda, as the importance of regimes invites participation by previously marginal actors. This will necessitate a period of adjustment for former systemic leaders; substantial stress is anticipated in their policy making apparatuses until their previous goals and preconceptions are brought into line with modern reality. Mistakes in setting goals and assigning means to achieving those objectives may be common until the objective and subjective situations are brought into rough equivalence.

Linking of issues. Because of the variety of types of power, and the number of actors with influence on the policy agenda, it may be difficult for states to link issues. States usually considered strong will have problems in this area; their greatest successes will come in dealings with other actors with whom it is mutually dependent, and in a number of issue areas. But because force is unusable, and actors can get resources from different places and actors, linkage of issues may more appropriately be considered a bonus, not something which can be intentionally pursued. More successful in economic and political terms will be states whose decision makers recognize these restrictions; if they do not policy failures can be especially costly in lost reputation.

Role of international organization. The role of international organizations has much to do with the variety of types of power in existence. In some organizations such as the UN, voting strength is sufficient for states which share goals to have power. In other organizations such as the IMF and the World Bank, other assets under the control of individual states equate with power. Participation may be high in organizations of both extremes, but states--especially those new to the understanding of complex interdependence--will reserve the right to opt out of the requirements of these organizations. This reflects the fact that complex interdependence does not expect states to surrender any sovereignty to multilateral bodies.

Chapters Six through Nine are case studies. As predicted by the above model, they report on the difficulty the Reagan Administration experienced in designing effective policies toward LDC debt. Generally speaking, the Administration found itself unable to exit a situation in which it was mutually dependent on a number of other actors for both its political and economic prosperity. Force was never a useful option, there were indeed multiple channels of contact, and for many actors in international debt the primary issue on their political agenda was financial, not territorial or military, security. And as predicted in the model of political processes in complex interdependence, many of the Administration's problems in leading an international response to the debt "crisis" stemmed from its tardy recognition of the magnitude of the problem and the number of actors threatened by it.

Chapter Six details Poland's financial problems in the early 1980s. It reviews Poland's struggle in 1981 to reschedule its debt due to Paris Club creditors and private banks. Evidence reveals U.S. money center banks nearly caused a Polish default, even while their European colleagues and the U.S. government strongly supported a more lenient policy toward Warsaw's obligations. This chapter also explains the Reagan Administration's decision not to force a Polish default on hundreds of millions of dollars of agricultural credits guaranteed by the Commodity Credit Corporation. In early 1982 Warsaw was well behind on its payments to U.S. banks which had extended funds to Poland, and normal procedures would have required a formal default call by banks before government reimbursement could be made. But despite its hard-line approach to Poland's martial law declaration of December 1981, the Reagan Administration quietly paid the overdue amounts without requiring a Polish default. The Administration was unwilling to incur the anger of more heavily exposed European banks and governments, and claimed that keeping Poland's "feet to the fire" was actually the tougher approach.

Chapter Seven relates the Reagan Administration's part in the Mexican "rescue" in late 1982, when Mexico came within days of a default on privately held debt. In its actions, the Administration demonstrated its need for the IMF's assistance in avoiding disaster, and engaged other developed states in a concerted response to the threat to the international economy. The rescue effort mounted for Mexico indicated the Administration could depart from its laissez-faire preconceptions if the need was sufficiently pronounced. The Mexican case is especially vital in attempting to comprehend international debt from a complex interdependence standpoint. It illustrates the variety of banks, creditor governments, MDBs, and debtor states which were involved in varying degrees, none of which could act unilaterally without expecting a response from other actors.

The Reagan Administration's incipient shift away from laissez-faire policies is further documented in Chapter Eight, which describes the U.S.' agreement to a substantial increase in the lending power of the IMF. As evidence indicates, Reagan officials, long suspicious of the type of international economic coordination fostered by the Fund, were compelled to agree to an increase in the organization's influence because of the burgeoning external debt situation. The Administration's recognition of the growing chances of LDC defaults prompted it to push through Congress its request for $8.4 billion in new funds as part of the U.S. quota for the IMF, despite heavy bipartisan opposition. In the end, the Administration was compelled to accept a $15.6 billion housing appropriation it opposed, just to get the IMF bill approved.

Finally, Chapter Nine summarizes the events prompting the Administration to promulgate the "Baker Plan". In the three years after the Mexican debt scare, and as the global economy grew, LDC fortunes first seemed to improve, and then fell back to their previously depressed state. By mid-1985 it was apparent to some in the Administration, including new personnel in the State and Treasury Departments, that a genuine threat of coordinated debt payments moratoriums existed. In hopes of forestalling that possibility, and stimulating new commercial bank lending, in October 1985 the Administration announced a three-year assistance plan for fifteen target LDCs. In exchange for free-market reforms in developing states, the U.S. said it would support $9 billion in lending above forecast levels by the World Bank and its affiliated organizations, and push for $20 billion in new loans by commercial banks. Through Treasury Secretary James Baker, who announced the plan at the annual IMF/World Bank meeting in Seoul, the U.S. implied it might support higher funding levels for the MDBs, if developing countries made the suggested structural economic reforms. The "Plan for Sustained Growth" was generally portrayed by outside observers as indicating that within the Administration 'pragmatism had replaced ideology'.

A Future for Complex Interdependence?

Among the reasons for conducting this study were desires to stimulate new thinking about complex interdependence, and to apply it more broadly than has been the case in the past. In the previous pages the value of Keohane and Nye's framework for interpreting the systemic politics of international debt has been demonstrated, and an attempt has been made to extend it to modeling foreign policy in nonrealist conditions. Utilizing the Reagan Administration's policies as test cases has been helpful, because the eagerness of Reagan and his subordinates to prove the validity of realist assumptions about the international system provides a strong challenge to the expectations suggested by complex interdependence. Nonetheless, it has been concluded that in international debt Keohane and Nye's model functions well as both an explanatory and predictive tool.

But the foreign policy model explicated in Chapter Five has only been given one test. Will it explain politics in other issue areas? As Keohane and Nye intimate in Power and Interdependence, and as I have done so here, the notion of complex interdependence pretends to have great scope. It therefore needs some improvement. One indispensable method of improving this framework is to look for evidence of complex interdependence in other issue areas. For example, Gardner (1988) develops a list of issues where "practical internationalism" might be in order. These, he says in language which reflects some of the fundamentals of complex interdependence, are areas in which policy makers "will need to blend power politics and world-order politics, unilateralism and multilateralism--acting alone where multilateral solutions are unavailable, [and] developing multilateral options where they represent better means" of reaching national objectives (1988:830). Gardner suggests that in addition to global trade and finance, where a more pragmatic line is obviously warranted, practical internationalism could be successful in pursuing goals in the areas of nuclear proliferation and nuclear energy, drug trafficking, AIDS, environmental problems, and population growth (1988:831-833). All of these areas are arguably prone to analysis through a complex interdependence framework; all presently or could entail sufficiently severe threats to national security to place them high on domestic (and international) political agendas. Short of applying the complex interdependence framework to other topics, however, there is much that can be done within in-ternational debt. Conceptually, the need exists for more precise measures of interdependence. This includes development of quantitative measures of interdependence, whose utilization would allow comparison and study of mutual dependence over time. Such discrete variables could then be correlated with indicators of <u>perceived</u> interdependence, to further the explanation of foreign policy making in such situations. Empirically, vital study can be done on the different perceptions of international debt which existed at different times within the Reagan Administration. And more information is needed on the actual and potential effects of debt defaults, since none has occurred recently. Without politically informed scenarios of these occurrences there is no way to know if the concern which permeates the international financial community over debt from time to time is completely justified.

In extending and utilizing Keohane and Nye's framework, the question arises: Is complex interdependence a new paradigm? That is, does it rank in complexity and status with realism, dependency theory, and global society models, the three paradigms discussed in Chapter One? One way to answer that question is to utilize Holsti's (1985) criteria for identifying paradigms in international relations.

"International theory", Holsti writes, "has traditionally revolved around three key questions, the first of which is absolutely essential, the <u>raison d'etre</u> of the field, with the other two providing the location for solutions to the problem". The three identifying criteria are "(1) the causes of war and the conditions of peace/security/order; an essential subsidiary problem is the nature of power; (2) the essential actors and/or units of analysis; (3) images of the world/system/society of states" (1985:7-8). In the "classical tradition"--realism--in international relations, Holsti writes, scholars study certain phenomena "because of deeply held normative concern about the problem of war", and because war "has been a major source of historical change". As for the second criterion, analysts in the classical tradition have always placed their major focus on nation-states, because they "share the legal attribute of sovereignty" and because they are the essential actors involved in creating the governing rules for the international system. Finally, in the classical tradition the image of the world is one of "sovereign states, each possessing the capacity to make war against each other, and all suffering in various degrees from the security dilemma" (1985:9-10).

It should be obvious that the conceptual and empirical foundations of complex interdependence differ significantly from those of the classical tradition as expressed by Holsti. First, as discussed so far, complex interdependence does not discount war as a concern, but deemphasises it on the hierarchy of interests. In this sense, complex interdependence differs from realism in that it is applicable in a variety of situations where political and military security are of reduced importance. As to the second criterion, complex interdependence expands the focus of research far beyond nation-states. As the discussion in this study shows, there are numerous instances in which non-state actors can control the political agenda and frustrate the policies of national governments. Third, complex interdependence does not necessarily deny the omnipresence of the "security dilemma", but sees security as existing on a variety of levels, influenced by various actors with divergent capabilities.

Therefore, as matters now stand, complex interdependence indeed does have some of the elements necessary to give it paradigmatic status. But if one were to forecast its future as an analytic tool, it would be safer to suggest it could be applied more often to the day-to-day dealings among international actors, while realism will continue to provide the framework for understanding broad, global security issues. And of course, until or unless complex interdependence gains widespread currency in the literature of international relations, it cannot be considered a challenger to realism.

At this point critics may wonder how Keohane and Nye view complex interdependence after more than a decade and a half of discussion. As originally conceived, this study was based on their ideas as published in 1977; for that reason it has worked without reference to analyses of their text by others (see for example Holsti, 1978), and have made only passing reference to a 1985 article in which Keohane and Nye view the Reagan Administration as moving away from its original positions and more toward multilateralism in a variety of issue areas. Therefore, it is somewhat gratifying to note evidence Keohane and Nye still support their original conclusions.

In 1989 the second edition of Power and Interdependence was published. Keohane and Nye pointedly decided not to change the text of their argument in any way. In the preface to the second edition, the authors acknowledge the impact of events of the 1970s on their analysis, and how some critics felt their conclusions were made obsolete by politics in the early 1980s. But despite the intervening years and events, Keohane and Nye say Power and Interdependence has fared well (1989:x-xi):

> Just as some analysts in the 1970s overstated the obsolecence (sic) of the nation state, the decline of force, and the irrelevance of security concerns, others in the early 1980s unduly neglected the role of transnational actors and economic interdependence. Contrary to the tone of much political rhetoric and some political analysis, however, the 1980s did not represent a return to the world of the 1950s. Just as the decline of American power was exaggerated in the 1970s, so was the restoration of American power exaggerated in the 1980s. Looking carefully at military and economic indices of power resources, one notes that there was far more change in psychology and mood than in true indicators of power resources. The diffusion of power continued as measured by shares in world trade or world product. Economic interdependence as measured by vulnerability to supply shocks eased in a period of slack commodity markets (but it could change if markets tighten again and growth of economic transactions continues). Sensitivity

to exchange-rate fluctuations remained high. The costs of the great powers' use of force remained higher than in the 1950s. Moreover, despite rhetoric, the relations between the superpowers did not show a return to the Cold War period. Not only were alliances looser, but transactions were higher and relations between the superpowers reflected a fair degree of learning in the nuclear area. In our view, therefore, the analysis that we put forward in Power and Interdependence has not been rendered irrelevant by events. The real questions are not about obsolescence, but about analytical cogency.

International Debt and U.S. Foreign Policy: What Now?

Although the Reagan Administration has been succeeded by the Bush Administration, the core of U.S. debt policy has remained largely the same: to resist any dramatic changes in the nature of the international economy, and to adopt small-scale initiatives for ending LDC external debt difficulties rather than to support any broad efforts to reform the global economic system. Unfortunately, within that approach the two major debt assistance plans the U.S. has announced in the last five years--the Baker and Brady Plans--have been unsuccessful.

During the three years the Baker Plan covered (1986-1988), new bank lending was to be the key to stimulating LDC economic expansion. But in that period banks only lent approximately $10 billion to developing states, an amount barely sufficient for debtor countries to maintain interest payments on previous loans (Pine, 1989a). That amount was only half the total suggested in the Plan, and clearly left no money free for development purposes. Banks continued their exit from the long-term debt market. In fact, during 1987 and 1988 only Brazil, Argentina, and Mexico received any new long-term bank funding (Islam, 1989:46).

During the three years of the Baker Plan, U.S. banks especially continued their mass exodus from LDC lending, reflecting both Reagan Administration impotence and disinterest in forcing new commitments of funds to developing states. In early 1989 the Comptroller of the Currency reported U.S. banks had reduced their exposure in "troubled" LDCs from $102 billion in 1982 to $81 billion in 1988. During the same period these banks doubled their capital from $58 billion to $116 billion. In 1982 collective U.S. bank exposure in LDCs was 176% of capital; by January 1989 the figure was 70%. In June 1988 the nine major U.S. lenders--Bank of America, Manufacturers Hanover, Continental Illinois, Bankers Trust, Morgan Guarantee, First Chicago, Chase Manhattan, Chemical Bank, and Citicorp--had $55 billion in outstanding loans to the six largest LDC borrowers--Argentina, Brazil, Chile, Mexico, the Philippines, and Venezuela--compared with $61 billion in 1983. During the same period, the capital totals of those banks rose from $32 billion to $65 billion (Rosenblatt, 1989:15).

Hakim (1986:55) has analyzed some of the reasons for the failure of the Baker Plan. He notes that from the start the new lending called for was insufficient for the stated purposes, and the reforms mandated in LDCs did not take into account the political and economic conditions in developing states. Moreover, he writes, the Plan did not deal with the effects of low commodity prices or high interest rates in developed states. It ignored the plight of relatively small debtors, and made no connection between the size of the U.S. budget deficit and interest rates which make LDC borrowing difficult.

Also, Hakim writes, despite the Plan's early reception by observers who believed it signified a major change in U.S. policy, there was actually little new in the initiative (1986:56). For example, debtor growth had long been seen as necessary for an enduring solution to LDC economic problems, with austerity only a temporary measure designed not to produce recovery, but to generate the foreign exchange needed for debt service and to avoid defaults. The need for greater efficiency and productivity in developing states was also generally recognized. And the goal of stimulating bank lending had been part of IMF policy for at least three years.

Hakim also points out there were a number of factors impeding new lending about which the Reagan Administration could do very little (1986:57). For example, while the Administration did not do much to force new lending by American banks, it had no effective influence over European or Japanese banks. With the Administration eager to get cooperation from its developed allies on issues of trade, interest rates, and exchange rates, new bank lending to developing states was demoted on the political agenda. And the debtor states themselves must take some responsibility for the failure of the Baker Plan, Hakim says. These states criticized some parts of the program, accepted others, but never produced an alternative initiative of their own or a concerted response to the U.S.' proposal.

In March 1989, the Bush Administration's Treasury Secretary Nicholas Brady announced another U.S. initiative to relieve the debt burden on developing states (Pine, 1989b). Whereas the Baker Plan emphasized new lending to LDCs, the Brady Plan focused on debt reduction. This program reflected the Bush Administration's desire to have commercial banks cancel or reduce a portion of the external debt of thirty-nine developing countries (Rowen, 1989). In many ways the Brady Plan was similar to the Baker Plan; it called for reform of LDC economies along capitalist lines, continued commercial bank lending, and an active role by creditor states in rescheduling LDC external debts. But one new idea was included. Developing states would sell long-term bonds to commercial banks, in exchange for which the banks would retire outstanding debts. These bond sales, to be guaranteed with collateral from the IMF and World Bank, would allow LDCs both to reduce their total debt and devote funds to development projects. A concomitant benefit would be that private banks, with their exposure reduced, might once again increase their lending to deserving states.

Over the short term, the Brady Plan fared little better than did the Baker Plan. By the spring of 1990, only three countries--Costa Rica, Mexico, and the Philippines--had benefitted from U.S. efforts, and all only to a marginal degree. The Philippine debt-relief package was actually accomplished in a separate arrangement sponsored by the State Department (Pine, 1990). The agreement between Mexico and its private creditors was estimated to have reduced the country's 1990 debt service burden by only $2 billion, leaving it with $12 billion in payments; that amount was forecast to be 45% of exports for the year (Schmidt and Stamos, 1990). Critics observed that the Brady Plan concentrated on the debt owed to banks, at a time when bank exposure had been declining, and did nothing to ease the burden imposed by variable interest rates on external debt (Islam, 1989:40-42). Perhaps most importantly, while the Baker Plan allowed private banks to list 100% of their loans as assets, no matter how questionable the stability of their debtors, under the Brady Plan banks were free to continue new lending or to exit lending in developed states altogether, no matter how badly those states needed funds (Pine, 1989c:3).

U.S. policy on international debt has now gone through three phases. From 1982 to 1985, LDC austerity was the chosen approach. From 1985 to 1989, new funding was emphasized. Since 1989 debt reduction has been the preferred option. This study has demonstrated the continuing inability of the U.S.--or any other actor, for that matter--to pursue unilateral policies in managing international debt. It has also shown that virtually all actors in the issue area stand to be affected by the policies of others. Complex interdependence provides a theoretical basis for explaining the patterns of interaction within international debt. It remains to be seen if related lessons can be drawn by decision makers.

REFERENCES

Alker, Hayward R. Jr. and Thomas J. Biersteker. 1984. "The Dialectics of World Order: Notes for a Future Archeologist of International Savior Faire." International Studies Quarterly 28 (June):121-142.

Ambrose, Stephen E. 1988. Rise to Globalism: American Foreign Policy Since 1938. New York: Penguin Books.

Amezegar, Jahangir. 1986. "The IMF Under Fire." Foreign Policy (Fall):98-119.

Anderson, William D. and Sterling J. Kernek. 1985. "How Realistic Is Reagan's Diplomacy?" Political Science Quarterly 100:389-409.

Ash, Timothy Garton. 1984. "Under Western Eyes: Poland, 1980-1982." Washington Quarterly 7:120-134.

Astiz, Carlos. 1983. "U.S. Policy in Latin America." Current History 82:49-51,87.

Atkinson, Caroline. 1981. "U.S. Banks Balk At Long Terms For Polish Debt." Washington Post (June 20):A1,18.

--------. 1983. "Senate Panel Readies Bill On IMF Loans." Washington Post (April 28):C1,3.

Auerbach, Stuart. 1983. "IMF Aid Linked to Steel Issue." Washington Post (August 2):E7,8.

Bagley, Bruce Michael. 1983. "Mexican Foreign Policy: The Decline of a Regional Power." Current History 82:406-409,437.

Baker, James A. III. 1986. "The Baker Plan," in Detlev Chr. Dicke, ed. Foreign Debts in the Present and a New International Economic Order. Fribourg (Switzerland): University Press.

"Baker's Half-baked Cake." 1985. Economist (October 19):15-16.

Balz, Don. 1983. "Democrats Ask Reagan To Disown GOP Attacks." Washington Post (August 20):A5.

"Bashing the IMF." 1983. Fortune (October 31):58.

Belaunde-Moreyra, Antonio. 1986. "Dramatic Action or Muddling Through Strategy in the Debt Problem," in Detlev Chr. Dicke, ed. Foreign Debts in the Present and a New International Economic Order. Fribourg (Switzerland): University Press.

Bennett, Robert A. 1981a. "U.S. Banks Seek A Delay In Talks on Polish Debts." New York Times (June 18):D1,13.

--------. 1981b. "Pact on Polish Debt Delayed." New York Times (July 3):D1,6.

--------. 1981c. "Poland Asks Foreign Banks' Help In Repayment of Overdue Interest." New York Times (December 17):A1,D14.

--------. 1982a. "Two Banks Downgrade Polish Debt." New York Times (January 15):D1,2.

--------. 1982b. "Mexico Seeking Postponement of Part of Debt." New York Times (August 20):A1,D15.

--------. 1982c. "Bankers Seek a Rise for IMF." New York Times (September 9):D1,25.

Bialer, Seweryn. 1981. "Poland and the Soviet Imperium." Foreign Affairs 59:522-539.

"Bill Hits New Snag." 1983. New York Times (September 16):D4.

"Billions In Aid Set to Insure Stable System." 1982. New York Times (August 31):D1,5.

Board of Governors. 1983. Federal Reserve Bulletin 69 (April).

Bodayla, Stephen D. 1982. "Bankers Versus Diplomats: The Debate Over Mexican Insolvency." Journal of Interamerican Studies and World Affairs 24:461-482.

Bogdanowicz-Bindert, Christine. 1985-1986. "World Debt: The United States Reconsiders." Foreign Affairs 64:259-273.

Bouchet, Michel Henri. 1987. The Political Economy of International Debt: What, Who, How Much, and Why? New York: Quorum Books.

Bourne, Eric. 1981. "U.S. Banks Deal Poles' Hand-to-Mouth Economy a Fresh Blow." Christian Science Monitor (June 17):7.

Bowers, Stephen R. 1982. "An Assessment of the Polish Crisis: The East European View." Journal of Social, Political, and Economic Studies 7:257-268.

Bromke, Adam. 1980-1981. "Poland: The Cliff's Edge." Foreign Policy (Winter):154-162.

Brown, Seyom. 1983. The Faces of Power: Constancy and Change in United States Foreign Policy from Truman to Reagan. New York: Columbia University Press.

"The Burns Cable." 1982. Wall Street Journal (February 5):26.

"Bushwhackers of the Bank Bailout." 1983. Fortune (August 8):32.

Canak, William L., ed. 1989. Lost Promises: Debt, Austerity, and Development in Latin America. Boulder (CO): Westview Press.

Caporaso, James and Stephen Haggard. 1989. "Power in the International Political Economy," in Richard J. Stoll and Michael D. Ward, eds. Power in World Politics. Boulder (CO): Lynne Rienner.

Carr, Edward Hallett. 1939. The Twenty Years' Crisis, 1919-1939: An Introduction to the Study of International Relations. New York: St. Martins.

Casteneda, Jorge. 1989. "Debt Fever Erupts." Los Angeles Times (March 8):K11.

"Change of Heart Toward the IMF." 1982. Business Week (December 20):70.

Clark, Timothy B. 1986. "Tackling the Debt Crisis." National Journal 18:1932-1939.

Claudon, Michael P., ed. 1986. World Debt Crisis: International Lending on Trial. Cambridge (MA): Ballinger Publishing.

Cline, William R. 1982-1983. "Mexico's Crisis, The World's Peril." Foreign Policy (Winter):107-118.

--------. 1984. International Debt: Systemic Risk and Policy Response. Washington (D.C.): Institute for International Economics.

Cody, Edward. 1982. "Polish Debt Renegotiation Suspended." Washington Post (January 16):A16.

Cohen, Benjamin J. 1985. "International Debt and Linkage Strategies: Some Foreign Policy Implications for the United States." in Miles Kahler, ed. The Politics of International Debt. Ithaca: Cornell University Press.

Conte, Christopher. 1983. "More U.S. Funds For IMF Cleared By Senate Panel." Wall Street Journal (April 29):3.

Cook, David T. 1983. "Beating the Drum Against More Aid for the IMF." Christian Science Monitor (September 28):9.

Cowan, Edward. 1982a. "U.S. to Pay Part of Polish Debt; Default Avoided." New York Times (February 1):A1,D3.

--------. 1982b. "Loans and Credits for Aiding Mexico Are Mapped by U.S." New York Times (August 21):A1,32.

Crittenden, Ann. 1980. "Banks Trim Loans to Third World Amid Fears of Repayment Problem." New York Times (April 14):A1,D3.

Cumings, Bruce. 1981. "Chinatown: Foreign Policy and Elite Realignment," in Thomas Ferguson and Joel Rogers, eds. The Hidden Election: Politics and Economics in the 1980 Presidential Election. New York: Pantheon Books.

Darity, William Jr. and Bobbie L. Horn. 1988. The Loan Pushers: The Role of Commercial Banks in the International Debt Crisis. Cambridge (MA): Ballinger Publishing.

The Debt Crisis Network. 1985. From Debt to Development: Alternatives to the International Debt Crisis. Washington (D.C.): Institute for Policy Studies.

"De-faulty Logic on Poland." 1982. Wall Street Journal (February 9):30.

"Delay Accepted On Polish Debt." 1981. New York Times (June 20):A34.

de Onis, Juan. 1981a. "Sharp Reduction Expected in Foreign Aid Request". New York Times (January 26):A7.

--------. 1981b. "Haig Fights Proposal for Drastic Reduction in Foreign Assistance." New York Times (January 31):A1,2.

--------. 1981c. "Primary Foreign Aid Survives in Budget." New York Times (February 22):A9.

Destler, I.M. 1982. "Reagan and Congress--Lessons of 1981." Washington Quarterly 5:3-15.

Diehl, Jackson. 1984. "Latin Americans Meet on Foreign Debt." Washington Post (June 22):D7,8.

Dougherty, James E. and Robert L. Pfaltzgraff. 1981. Contending Theories of International Relations: A Comprehensive Survey. Second edition. New York: Harper and Row.

Ellis, Harry B. 1983. "Volcker Choice A Boost for Allies, Wall Street--and the President." Christian Science Monitor (June 20):1,9.

Evans, Richard. 1986. "Finance Minister of the Year: Baker." Euromoney (September):90-91,93.

Fagen, Richard R. 1984. "United States Policy in Central America." Millenium: Journal of International Studies 13:105-115.

Fallenbuchl, Zbigniew. 1982. "Poland's Economic Crisis." Problems of Communism 31:1-21.

Farnsworth, Clyde. 1981a. "Reagan Cautions Developing Lands On Economic Help." New York Times (September 30):A1,D22.

--------. 1981b. "Foreign Aid Donors Set Cutbacks." New York Times (October 1):D1,13.

--------. 1981c. "Reagan Bids Third World Adopt Free Enterprise to Battle Poverty." New York Times (October 16):A1,2.

--------. 1981d. "U.S. May Cut Poor Nations Loan Aid." New York Times (November 25):D2.

--------. 1982a. "Poland Reported Paying Debt Unaided by Soviets." New York Times (January 28):D1,3.

--------. 1982b. "Polish Debt Payments to U.S. Cited." New York Times (February 24):D6.

--------. 1982c. "Loans to Poor Countries May Rise $500 Million." New York Times (April 6):D1.

--------. 1982d. "U.S. Backs Decision To Raise IMF Aid to Poor Countries." New York Times (September 5):A1,13.

--------. 1982e. "House Panel Criticizes Plan to Raise IMF Aid." New York Times (December 22):D1,3.

--------. 1982f. "IMF Loan to Mexico." New York Times (December 24):D4.

--------. 1983a. "$32.5 Billion Rise In Loan Program Approved By IMF." New York Times (February 12):A1,31.

--------. 1983b. "House Unit Would Curb IMF Loans to Pretoria." New York Times (May 6):D1,6.

--------. 1983c. "Senate Conservatives Fight IMF Fund Rise." New York Times (June 7):D11.

--------. 1983d. "Senate Defeats Curbs On IMF Bill." New York Times (June 8):D1,10.

--------. 1983e. "$8.4 Billion Approved For IMF." New York Times (June 9):D1,16.

--------. 1983f. "Hard Fight Expected On IMF." New York Times (September 12):D1,9.

--------. 1983g. "U.S. Urging Curbs On Loans By IMF To Poor Countries." New York Times (September 26):A1,D5.

--------. 1983h. "Brazil To Receive $11 Billion In Aid." New York Times (September 27):A1,D6.

--------. 1983i. "Reagan Praises IMF and Warns Congress Over Delays in New Aid." New York Times (September 28):A1,D27.

--------. 1983j. "Reagan Thanks Democrats." New York Times (October 25):D1,17.

--------. 1983k. "Senate Votes IMF Increase." New York Times (November 18):D1,7.

--------. 1984. "31 Countries to Donate $9 Billion To World Bank Agency for Poor." New York Times (January 15):A1,13.

--------. 1985a. "U.S. to Propose New Effort to Ease Debt Crisis." New York Times (September 21):A41.

--------. 1985b. "U.S. Said To Urge More Assistance For Third World." New York Times (October 6):A1,13.

--------. 1985c. "U.S. May Back Higher Lending By World Bank." New York Times (October 7):A1,10.

--------. 1985d. "Bankers At IMF Talks Cautious On Baker Plan." New York Times (October 9):D1,22.

Fatemi, Khosrow, ed. 1988. International Trade and Finance: A North American Perspective. New York: Praeger.

Fischer, Stanley. 1987. "Resolving the International Debt Crisis." NBER Working Paper Series. (September) Cambridge (MA): National Bureau of Economic Research.

Fishlow, Albert. 1986. "Lessons From the Past: Capital Markets During the 19th Century and the Interwar Period," in Miles Kahler, ed. The Politics of International Debt. Ithaca: Cornell University Press.

"Foreign Aid Study Favors Private Enterprise." 1982. New York Times (January 2):A5.

Fouquet, David. 1981. "Banks Agree to Give Weary Poles a Grace Period to Pay Back Huge Debt." Christian Science Monitor (July 24):10.

Francis, David R. 1983. "Congress Balks On Upping U.S. Help for Have-Not Nations." Christian Science Monitor (September 29):8.

Frieden, Jeff. 1981. "Third World Indebted Industrialization: International Finance and State Capitalization in Mexico, Brazil, Algeria, and South Korea." International Organization 35:407-431.

Friedman, Thomas L. 1981. "Banks and U.S. Officials Hopeful on Polish Debts." New York Times (December 15):A21.

Fuerenberger, Jonathan. 1983a. "House Unit Votes Aid for IMF." New York Times (May 10):D1,17.

--------. 1983b. "Reagan Urges the House to Back IMF Increase." New York Times (July 20):D1,26.

--------. 1983c. "House Move May Hurt Chances for IMF Bill." New York Times (July 27):D1,4.

--------. 1983d. "Revised IMF Bill Attracts Support." New York Times (July 29):D1,5.

--------. 1983e. "House, 217-211, Approves Rise In U.S. Contribution to the IMF." New York Times (August 4):A1,D21.

Gaddis, John Lewis. 1982. Strategies of Containment: A Critical Appraisal of Postwar American National Security Policy. Oxford: Oxford University Press.

Gailey, Phil. 1982. Polish Debts: Extent of the U.S. Liability." New York Times (February 6):A29,38.

"A Game of Chicken Over Funding for the IMF." 1983. Business Week (October 31):49.

Gardner, Richard N. 1988. "The Case for Practical Internationalism." Foreign Affairs 66:827-845.

Gelb, Leslie. 1982. "Reprieve on Polish Debt." New York Times (February 3):A1,9.

Gilpin, Kenneth N. 1981. "The IMF Gathers in Gabon." New York Times (May 15):C1.

--------. 1983a. "World Debt Refinancing And Its Impact on Banks." New York Times (June 18):A29,35.

--------. 1983b. "Stretching Out Mexico's Debt." New York Times (August 27):A33,37.

Gilpin, Robert. 1981. War and Change in World Politics. Cambridge: Cambridge University Press.

Glennon, Michael, Diane Granat, and Robert Rothman. 1983. "IMF-Housing Bargain Cleared By End-of-Session Packaging." CQ Weekly Report 41:2457-2458.

Gwertzman, Bernard. 1980. "Carter Decides to Defer Action On Aid to Poles." New York Times (November 22):A1,6.

Haggard, Stephen. 1986. "The Politics of Adjustment: Lessons From the IMF's External Fund Facility," in Miles Kahler, ed. The Politics of International Debt. Ithaca: Cornell University Press.

Haig, Alexander M. Jr. 1981. "A New Direction In U.S. Foreign Policy." The Atlantic Quarterly 19:131-137.

Hailey, Richard M. 1981. "Confusing White House Signals Peril International Lending Agencies." Christian Science Monitor (June 25):4.

Hakim, Peter. 1986. "The Baker Plan: Unfulfilled Promises." Challenge 29:55-59.

Harrison, Michael M. 1981. "Reagan's World." Foreign Policy (Summer):3-16.

Hartland-Thunberg, Penelope. 1986. "Causes and Consequences of the World Debt Crisis," in Penelope Hartland-Thunberg and Charles K. Ebinger, eds. Banks, Petrodollars, and Sovereign Debtors: Blood from a Stone? Lexington (MA): Lexington Books.

Hartland-Thunberg, Penelope and Charles K. Ebinger. 1986. "Mexico's Economic Anguish," in Penelope Hartland-Thunberg and Charles K. Ebinger, eds. Banks, Petrodollars, and Sovereign Debtors: Blood from a Stone? Lexington (MA): Lexington Books.

Hassner, Pierre. 1981. "New Centers of Weakness: Beyond Power and Interdependence." Social Research 48:677-699.

Hoffman, Stanley. 1981. "Notes on the Limits of 'Realism'." Social Research 48:653-659.

Holsti, K.J. 1978. "A New International Politics? Diplomacy In Complex Interdependence." International Organization 32:513-530.

--------. 1985. The Dividing Discipline: Hegemony and Diversity in International Theory. Boston: Allen & Unwin.

Hosendolph, Ernest. 1983. "U.S. Dunning Is 'Not Nasty'." New York Times (March 4):D2.

Hudes, Karen. 1985. "Coordination of Paris and London Club Reschedulings." New York University Journal of International Law and Politics 17:553-571.

Hunt, Michael. 1987. Ideology and U.S. Foreign Policy. New Haven: Yale University Press.

"IMF Funds Increased, EX-IM Bank Extended." 1983. CQ Almanac. pp. 241-248. Washington (DC): Congressional Quarterly.

"The IMF Is Alive and Well And Counting On Congress." 1983. Economist (October 1):65-66.

"IMF Loan Cutback Seen." 1983. New York Times (September 23):D11.

"The IMF Orders Banks to Keep Mexico Afloat." 1982. Business Week (December 6):34-35.

Ipson, Erik. 1985. "Can the Baker Plan Work?" Institutional Investor 19:279-286.

Islam, Shafiqul. 1987. "America's Foreign Debt: Is the Debt Crisis Moving North?" Stanford Journal of International Law 23:99-129.

--------. 1989. "Going Beyond the Brady Plan." Challenge 32:39-46.

"It's High Noon for IMF Funding." 1983. Business Week (October 3):40-41.

Kahler, Miles., ed. 1986a. The Politics of International Debt. Ithaca: Cornell University Press.

--------. 1986b. "Politics and International Debt: Explaining the Debt Crisis," in Miles Kahler, ed. The Politics of International Debt. Ithaca: Cornell University Press.

Kaufman, Robert R. 1986. "Democratic and Authoritarian Responses to the Debt Issue: Argentina, Brazil, Mexico," in Miles Kahler, ed. The Politics of International Debt. Ithaca: Cornell University Press.

Kegley, Charles W. Jr. and Eugene R. Wittkopf. 1982. "The Reagan Administration's World View." Orbis 26:223-244.

--------. 1987. American Foreign Policy: Pattern and Process. Third edition. New York: St. Martins.

Kempe, Frederick. 1982. "Poland's 'Default Day' Passes in Silence As Bankers Wrestle With Woes Elsewhere." Wall Street Journal (September 13):35.

Keohane, Robert O. and Joseph S, Nye, Jr., eds. 1971. "Transnational Relations and World Politics." International Organization 25.

--------. 1977. Power and Interdependence: World Politics in Transition. Boston: Little, Brown.

--------. 1985. "Two Cheers for Multilateralism." Foreign Policy (Fall):148-167.

--------. 1989. Power and Interdependence: World Politics in Transition. Second edition. Boston: Scott, Foresman.

Kettell, Brian and George Magnus. 1986. The International Debt Game. London: Graham and Trotman Limited.

Kilborn, Peter T. 1985a. "Baker and Volcker Ask Bank Aid on Debt Woes." New York Times (October 2):D12.

--------. 1985b. "Role of World Bank Seen As Enchanced." New York Times (October 3):D6.

--------. 1985c. "Administration Is Adopting Assertive Economic Stance." New York Times (October 7):A10.

Kindleberger, Charles P. 1981. "Dominance and Leadership in the International Economy: Exploitation, Public Goods, and Free Riders." International Studies Quarterly 25:242-254.

King, Seth S. 1982a. "U.S. to Pay $138 Million To Banks on Polish Aid." New York Times (April 20):D1,14.

--------. 1982b. "Polish Loan Claims Up $52 Million." New York Times (June 15):D16.

Kraft, Joseph. 1984. The Mexican Rescue. New York: Group of Thirty.

Krazenbuehl, Thomas C. 1986. "Comecon As a Debtor of the Western Financial System," in Detlev Chr. Dicke, ed. Foreign Debts in the Present and a New International Economic Order. Fribourg (Switzerland): University Press.

Kuczynski, Pedro-Pablo. 1983. "Why the Music Stopped." Challenge 25:20-29.

--------. 1988. Latin American Debt. Baltimore: Johns Hopkins University Press.

Kurtz, Howard. 1983. "Massive IMF, Housing Compromise Is Approved by Senate, 67-30: House Expected to Concur Today." Washington Post (November 18):D8,11.

"Learning How to Count Foreign Aid." 1981. New York Times (February 4):A22.

Lewis, Paul. 1981a. "West Allows Poles 4-Year Debt Delay." New York Times (April 28):D1,18.

--------. 1981b. "Banks in Compromise To Defer Polish Debt." New York Times (June 26):D1,9.

--------. 1981c. "Banks Said to Reject Polish Bid for Loan." New York Times (December 23):D2.

--------. 1982a. "Poland Said to Threaten Default if Aid is Denied." New York Times (June 6):D1,3.

--------. 1982b. "U.S. Is Said To Support IMF Rise." New York Times (December 5):D1,2.

--------. 1983a. "$20 Billion Aid Accord For IMF." New York Times (January 18):D1,15.

--------. 1983b. "Allies Pressing U.S. on IMF Bill." New York Times (September 16):D4.

Lipsky, Seth. 1982. "Officials Argue U.S. Role on Polish Debt." Wall Street Journal (January 7):20.

Lipson, Charles. 1981. "The International Organization of Third World Debt." International Organization 35:603-631.

--------. 1985. "Bankers Dilemmas: Private Cooperation in Rescheduling Sovereign Debts." World Politics 38:200-225.

"Living With A Nightmare." 1982. Economist (March 20):9-10.

Long, Millard and Frank Venereso. 1981. "The Debt Related Problems of the Non-Oil Less Developed Countries." Economic Development and Cultural Change 29:501-510.

Loomis, Carol J. 1985. "Why Baker's Debt Plan Won't Work." Fortune (December 23):98-102.

Macnamar, R.T. 1982. "Squeezing Poland." Washington Post (June 10):A17.

Maghroori, Ray and Bennett Ramberg, eds. 1982. Globalism Versus Realism: International Relations' Third Debate. Boulder (CO): Westview.

Makin, John H. 1984. The Global Debt Crisis: America's Growing Involvement. New York: Basic Books.

Mansbach, Richard W. and John A. Vasquez. 1981. In Search of Theory: A New Paradigm for Global Politics. New York: Columbia University Press.

Martin, Douglas. 1982. "Views Clash on World Bank Agency." New York Times (September 8):D6.

Martin, Sarah. 1981. "The Secrets of the Polish Memorandum." Euromoney (August):9-10,12,14-15.

McCormick, James M. 1984. "The NIEO and the Distribution of American Assistance." Western Political Quarterly 37:100-119.

Meissner, Charles F. 1984. "Debt: Reform Without Governments." Foreign Policy (Fall):81-93.

"Mexico Invites IMF." 1982. New York Times (August 17):D13.

Miller, Marjorie. 1989. "Mexico Balances Growth, Solvency in Negotiating Debt Plan." Los Angeles Times (March 23):D5.

Modelski, George. 1964. "Kautilya: Foreign Policy and International System in the Ancient Hindu World." American Political Science Review 53:549-560.

Morgan, Dan. 1982a. "West Faces Dilemma on Polish Debt." Washington Post (January 11):A15,19.

--------. 1982b. "U.S. Tells Its Banks Some Polish Debts Will Be Paid." Washington Post (February 2):A11.

Morgan, Dan and Margot Hornblower. 1982. "House Defeats Try to Override Administration's Polish Policy." Washington Post (February 10):A18.

Morgenthau, Hans J. 1948 (1973). Politics Among Nations: The Struggle for Power and Peace. Fifth edition. New York: Knopf.

Most, Benjamim A. and Harvey Starr. 1984. "International Relations Theory, Foreign Policy Substitutability, and 'Nice' Laws." World Politics 36:383-406.

"A New Crunch for Third World Debt." 1984. Business Week (April 28):28-29.

Newfarmer, Richard. 1983. "A Look at Reagan's Revolution in Development Policy." Challenge 26:34-43.

Oberdorfer, Don. 1980. "Hard-Pressed Poland Has Asked U.S. for $3 Billion in Emergency Aid." Washington Post (November 14):A14.

--------. 1981. "U.S. to Let Poland Defer Repaying $80 Million Debt." Washington Post (February 23):A1,6.

Oliver, James K. 1982. "The Balance of Power Heritage of 'Interdependence' and 'Traditionalism'." International Studies Quarterly 26:373-396.

"O'Neill--Reagan Dispute Over IMF Continues." 1983. New York Times (October 20):D21.

"Panel Approves IMF Funds." 1983. New York Times (April 29):D3.

Pine, Art. 1981a. "Reagan Voices 'Strong' Support for IMF, World Bank Despite Recent U.S. Criticism." Wall Street Journal (September 30):5.

--------. 1981b. "IMF and World Bank Conclude Meeting, Prepare to Tighten Loan Requirements." Wall Street Journal (October 5):34.

--------. 1983a. "U.S. Hints Acceptance of Move to Ease Global Woes Through the IMF." Wall Street Journal (January 20):2.

--------. 1983b. "House Unit Seen Backing Curbs On Loans Abroad." Wall Street Journal (February 3):2.

--------. 1983c. "IMF Debates 50% Boost in Loan Funds, But Congress Wary of U.S. Participation." Wall Street Journal (February 7):26.

--------. 1983d. "House Unit Spars With Bankers." New York Times (February 9):D7.

--------. 1983e. "IMF Near Accord on Quota Rise." New York Times (February 11):D1,4.

--------. 1983f. "Strange Bedfellows: Increased Aid to IMF Becomes Political Issue Crossing Party Lines." Wall Street Journal (September 26):1,21.

--------. 1988. "Bush Signals Strategy Change on Foreign Debt." Los Angeles Times (December 20):A1,19.

--------. 1989a. "Banks Offer Own Plan for Reducing Third World Debt." Los Angeles Times (January 12):D1,6.

--------. 1989b. "Treasury Chief Offers Plan to Ease Third World Debt." Los Angeles Times (March 11):A1,22.

--------. 1989c. "Brady Plan at Risk as Banks Balk at Third World Loans." Los Angeles Times (September 27):D1,3).

--------. 1990. "U.S. Makes Another Stab at Debt Relief for Mexico." Los Angeles Times (January 9).

"Poland: A Millstone of Debt Drags Warsaw Down." 1981. Business Week (July 7):53.

"Poland Said to Produce Cash to Avoid A Default." 1982. New York Times (January 4):A8.

"Poland Said to Reduce Bank Debt." 1982. New York Times (February 11):D10.

Polanyi, Karl. 1957. The Great Transformation. Boston: Beacon Press.

"The Polish Bogey." 1982. Economist (March 20):10,15-16,21-22.

"Polish Debt Due in '82 Is Deferred." 1982. New York Times (November 4):D15.

"Polish Debt Effect Cited." 1981. New York Times (October 2):D13.

"Polish Debt Extension." 1981. New York Times (July 24):D10.

"Polish Debt Talks Gain." 1981. New York Times (November 21):A39.

Pollin, Robert and Eduardo Zepeda. 1988. "Latin American Debt: The Choices Ahead," in Kofi Buenor Hadjor, ed. New Perspectives In North-South Dialogue: Essays in Honour of Olof Palme. London: I.B. Tauris & Co. Ltd.

Portes, Richard. 1981. "Poland and U.S. Bankers." New York Times (June 19):A27.

Poznansi, Kazimierz. 1986. "Economic Adjustment and Political Forces: Poland Since 1970." International Organization 40:455-488.

Purcell, Susan Kaufman. 1983a. "War and Debt In South America." Foreign Affairs 61:660-674.

--------. 1983b. "Latin American Debt and U.S. Economic Policy." Orbis 27:591-602.

"Questions Created on Polish Debt." 1981. New York Times (December 14):D1,4.

"Queue At the IMF." 1981. Economist (November 14):87.

"Reagan Asks Congress to Let Agencies Set Details of Limits on Bank Lending Abroad." 1983. Wall Street Journal (February 15):6.

"Reagan Is Set to Clip the IMF's Wings." 1981. Business Week (September 28):29.

"Reagan Takes His Policies Global." 1981. Business Week (October 12):42-43.

Regan, Donald T. 1983. "The United States and the World Debt Problem." Wall Street Journal (February 8):32.

Research and Policy Committee of the Committee for Economic Development. 1988. Finance and Third World Economic Growth. Boulder (CO): Westview Press.

Riding, Alan. 1982a. "Mexico's Road to Trouble Is Coated With Oil." New York Times (February 21):E3.

--------. 1982b. "Mexican Outlook: Banks Are Wary." New York Times (August 17):D1,13.

--------. 1982c. "Mexico Sets Talks On Its Debt." New York Times (August 19):D13.

--------. 1982d. "Mexico Agrees to Austerity Terms For $3.9 Billion in IMF Credit." New York Times (November 11):A1,D3.

--------. 1982e. "Credit for Mexico Is Reported." New York Times (November 19):D4.

--------. 1984. "Latin Debtors Seek a Strategy." New York Times (January 20):D1,2.

--------. 1985. "U.S. Shift On Latin Debt Seen As a Turning Point in Crisis." New York Times (October 3):A1,D6.

Roberts, Steven V. 1983a. "Trouble Seen In House for IMF Bill." New York Times (July 26):D3.

--------. 1983b. "Congress Finishes Pentagon Budget and Ends Session." New York Times (November 19):1,12.

Rosenau, James N. 1966 (1980). The Scientific Study of Foreign Policy. London: Frances Pinter Publishers.

--------. 1980. "Muddling, Meddling, and Modelling: Alternative Approaches to the Study of World Politics in an Era of Rapid Change." Millenium: Journal of International Studies 8:130-144.

Rosenblatt, Robert A. 1989. "Banks Seen as No Longer Imperiled by Foreign Debt." Los Angeles Times (January 6):A1,15.

Rowe, James L., Jr. 1981. "Poland Asks $350 Million From Its Major Creditors For Interest on Old Debts." Washington Post (December 17):D14,18.

--------. 1983a. "Administration Urges Help for IMF." <u>Washington Post</u> (July 20):D7,16.

--------. 1983b. "Volcker Urges House to Pass IMF Increase." <u>Washington Post</u> (July 21):B8.

Rowen, Hobart. 1981a. "U.S. Reviewing Its Development Institutions Role." <u>Washington Post</u> (February 21):D8,9.

--------. 1981b. "Regan Supports Tighter Lending To Third World." <u>Washington Post</u> (September 22):A1,6.

--------. 1981c. "Stress Free Enterprise, Reagan Tells Poor Lands." <u>Washington Post</u> (September 30):A3.

--------. 1982. "Regan Rejects IMF Doubling of Quotas." <u>Washington Post</u> (September 2):C13.

--------. 1983a. "U.S. Lags in Payments to World Bank Fund." <u>Washington Post</u> (January 28):A16.

--------. 1983b. "Schultz Deftly Tackles the Global Debt Crisis." <u>Washington Post</u> (February 27):F1,11.

--------. 1983c. "IDA Funds Seen in Trouble." <u>Washington Post</u> (March 10):E1,2.

--------. 1983d. "Fed Chief Criticizes Move That Could Limit IMF." <u>Washington Post</u> (July 18):A1,9.

--------. 1983e. "Substitute Bill On IMF Funds Finds Favor." <u>Washington Post</u> (July 29):C8,10.

--------. 1983f. "Massive IMF, Housing Compromise Is Approved by Senate, 67-30: Major Changes Seen In Lending." <u>Washington Post</u> (November 18):D8,11.

--------. 1985a. "World Bank Support in Question." <u>Washington Post</u> (May 12):F1,9.

--------. 1985b. "Washington's Changing Attitude." <u>Institutional Investor</u> 19:355-356,358.

--------. 1986. "Jim Baker's Global Blueprint." <u>Institutional Investor</u> 20:302-304,307,309-310.

--------. 1989. "Is It Time for A 'Debt Czar'?" <u>Washington Post</u> (December 28):A23.

Sachs, Jeffrey D. 1986. "Managing the LDC Debt Crisis." <u>Brookings Papers On Economic Activity</u> 2:397-431.

--------. ed. 1989. Developing Country Debt and the World Economy. Chicago: University of Chicago Press.

Samuels, Nathaniel. 1986. "Dealing With the International Debt Issue," in Penelope Hartland-Thunberg and Charles K. Ebinger, eds. Banks, Petrodollars, and Sovereign Debtors: Blood from a Stone? Lexington (MA): Lexington Books.

Schatan, Jacobo. 1988. "Debt and Dependency: The Case of Latin America," in Chadwick Alger and Michael Stoll, eds. A Just Peace Through Transformation: Cultural, Economic, and Political Foundations for Change. Boulder (CO): Westview Press.

Schmidt, Samuel and Stephen Stamos. 1990. "Nickeled-and-Dimed Deeper Into Debt." Los Angeles Times (February 14):B7.

Schultz, George. 1982. "U.S. Foreign Policy: Realism and Progress," in Marlow Reddleman, ed. U.S. Foreign Policy. New York: H.W. Wilson.

Seib, Gerald F. 1982. "Reagan's Opposition to Declaring Poland In Default Is Forcefully Defended by Aides." Wall Street Journal (February 24):4.

Seligman, Daniel. 1980. "Poland Might Be Only the Beginning." Fortune (December 1):103-104,108-109,112.

Silk, Leonard. 1981. "Reagan's Aims On Poor Lands." New York Times (October 2):D1.

--------. 1983. "Economic Scene: The Campaign Against the IMF." New York Times (October 19):D2.

Sjaastad, Larry A. 1983. "International Debt Quagmire--to Whom Do We Owe It?" World Economy 6:305-324.

Smith, Hedrik. 1982a. "Reagan Forced By Events Abroad to Temper His Hard-Line Policies." New York Times (January 22):A1,8.

--------. 1982b. "Weinberger Seeks to Declare Poles in Default on Debt." New York Times (February 4):A1,5.

Soloman, Julie. 1982. "Washington Talk of Polish Loan Default Has Made Western Lenders Very Nervous." Wall Street Journal (February 5):5.

"Soviet Bloc's Debts Worry Banks." 1980. New York Times (September 2):A16.

Spero, Joan Edelman. 1985. The Politics of International Economic Relations. New York: St. Martins.

Stallings, Barbara. 1987. Banker to the Third World: U.S. Portfolio Investment in Latin America, 1900-1986. Berkeley: University of California Press.

Stallings, Barbara and Robert Kaufman, eds. 1989. Debt and Democracy in Latin America. Boulder (CO): Westview Press.

Stein, Herbert. 1984. Presidential Economics: the Making of Economic Policy from Roosevelt to Reagan and Beyond. New York: Simon and Schuster.

Stoga, Alan J. 1986. "If America Won't Lead." Foreign Policy (Fall):79-97.

Stout, Richard L. 1983. "The Call Goes Out for Collective Action to Solve World Debt Crisis." Christian Science Monitor (April 18):4.

Strausz-Hupe, Robert. 1981. "Poland's Proletarian Revolution." Policy Review 15:61-69.

Sundaram, Jomo. 1988. "Third World Debt Bondage," in Chadwick Alger and Michael Stoll, eds. A Just Peace Through Transformation: Cultural, Economic, and Political Foundations for Change. Boulder (CO): Westview Press.

Tagliabue, John. 1980. "West Germans Plan Loan to Poland." New York Times (August 13):D6.

--------. 1981a. "Bonn Reportedly Agrees to Back Loans to Poland." New York Times (January 6):D1,11.

--------. 1981b. "German Banks Aid Poles." New York Times (April 16):D8.

--------. 1981c. "Poles In Accord on Bank Debt." New York Times (December 5):A34.

--------. 1981d. "German Banks Seek Bonn Pledge on Poland." New York Times (December 21):D1,2.

--------. 1981e. "Poles Make Small Debt Payments." New York Times (December 30):D1,5.

--------. 1982a. "Official Says Poland Will Pay Its Debts." New York Times (January 1):A38.

--------. 1982b. "Payments Reported By Poland." New York Times (January 13):D1,19.

--------. 1982c. "Banks Pressing Poland." New York Times (March 3):D3.

--------. 1982d. "Repayment by Poland Postponed." New York Times (April 7):D1,9.

--------. 1983. "Banks Reschedule Debt Due From Poland in '83." New York Times (August 19):D1,2.

"Third World Debt: It's the Fed Vs. the Bankers." 1984. Business Week (January 9):47.

Thompson, Kenneth W. 1952. "The Study of International Politics: A Survey of Trends and Developments." Review of International Politics 14:433-443.

"The Threat of Turmoil In Mexico." 1982. Business Week (September 13):104,106.

"Two Reagans and the IMF." Economist (June 18):16.

Tyson, Laura D'Andrea. 1986. "The Debt Crisis and Adjustment Responses in Eastern Europe: A Comparative Perspective." International Organization 40:239-285.

"U.S. Lets Poland Defer Payments." 1981. New York Times (February 27):A3.

"U.S. Plans to Cut Contribution To Loans for Poor Countries." 1982. New York Times (February 19):A6.

"U.S. Reported Planning to Defer Polish Debts." 1981. Christian Science Monitor (February 24):2.

"U.S. to Repay Polish Debt Without Default Statement." 1982. Christian Science Monitor (February 2):2.

Vasquez, John A. 1983. The Power of Power Politics: A Critique. New Brunswick (NJ): Rutgers University Press.

--------. ed. 1986. Evaluating U.S. Foreign Policy. New York: Praeger Special Studies.

Vernon, Raymond and Debora L. Spar. 1989. Beyond Globalism: Remaking American Foreign Economic Policy. New York: Free Press.

"Volcker Meets With Creditors On Brazil Debt." 1983. Wall Street Journal (June 3):25.

Waltz, Kenneth N. 1959. Man, the State, and War: A Theoretical Analysis. New York: Columbia University Press.

--------. 1979. Theory of International Politics. New York: Random House.

Wasowski, Stanislaw S. 1986. "U.S. Sanctions Against Poland." Washington Quarterly 9:167-184.

Webbe, Stephen. 1981. "Poland's Debts: West's Lever?" Christian Science Monitor (February 3):6.

Weinert, Richard S. 1986-1987. "Swapping Third World Debt." Foreign Policy (Winter):85-97.

Wellons, Phillip A. 1986. "International Debt: The Behavior of Banks In A Politicized Environment," in Miles Kahler, ed. The Politics of International Debt. Ithaca: Cornell University Press.

Wesson, Robert., ed. 1988. Coping With the Latin American Debt. New York: Praeger.

"Western Banks Ironing Out an Easing of Polish Debts." 1981. Christian Science Monitor (May 21):2.

"West Eyes Way to Ease Polish Debt." 1981. Washington Post (February 26): A31.

"West Grants Delay of Debt Payments by Hard-Pressed Poland." 1981. Washington Post (April 26):A16.

"The West's Stake in Poland." 1981. Business Week (December 28):48-49.

Whiting, Cyril R. 1980. "Soviets' Additional Help to Poland Expected to Tighten Economic Link." New York Times (September 14):A1.

Wiarda, Howard J. 1986. "The Paralysis of Policy: Current Dilemmas of U.S. Foreign Policy Making." World Affairs 149:15-20.

--------. 1987. "United States Relations with South America." Current History 86:1-4,35-36.

--------. 1988. "Can the Mice Roar? Small Countries and the Debt Crisis," in Robert Wesson, ed. Coping With the Latin American Debt. New York: Praeger.

Williams, Juan. "Reagan Backs Extra IMF Funds." Washington Post (July 24):A3.

Wolfe, Alan. 1986. "Crackpot Moralism, Neo-Realism, and U.S. Foreign Policy." World Policy Journal 3:251-275.

Wood, Robert E. 1986. From Marshall Plan to Debt Crisis: Foreign Aid and Development Choices in the World Economy. Berkeley: University of California Press.

"World Economics: Candidates Are Poles Apart." 1980. Business Week (November 10):125, 129.

Yochelson, John, ed. 1988. Keeping Pace: U.S. Policies and Global Economic Change. Cambridge (MA): Ballinger Publishing.

189

INDEX